IRRATIONAL
Economics

HOW TO SURVIVE & PROSPER
FROM THE FUNDAMENTAL FORCE
THAT REALLY DRIVES THE MARKETS

RODNEY JOHNSON

Delray Publishing
55 NE 5th Avenue 2nd Floor
Delray Beach FL, 33483
Phone: 1-888-211-2215
www.dentresearch.com

ISBN: 978-0-615-99307-2

Printed in the United States of America

To my lovely wife, Brook, and my children, Jacob, Nora, and Mollie. Being a spouse and a parent keeps me striving to know more by constantly reminding me of how much of the world I don't yet understand.

RODNEY JOHNSON

Rodney Johnson works closely with Harry S. Dent, Jr. to study how people spend their money as they go through predictable stages of life, how that spending drives our economy and how you can use this information to invest successfully in any market.

He began his career in financial services on Wall Street in the 1980s, with Thomson McKinnon and then Prudential Securities. He started working on projects with Harry in the mid-1990s.

He's a regular guest on several radio programs such as America's Wealth Management and Savvy Investor Radio, and he has been featured on CNBC, Fox News and Fox Business's America's Nightly Scorecard, where he discusses economic trends ranging from the price of oil to the direction of the U.S. economy.

He holds degrees from Georgetown University and Southern Methodist University.

*With this book of key issues by
Rodney, you can get to know his
unique and practical insights from
our demographic research —
you won't be disappointed!*

—Harry S. Dent, Jr.

TABLE OF CONTENTS

INTRODUCTION

Really?

Can I really make a zillion dollars by having my dog pick stocks? Can I make $1,000, $2,000, or even up to $3,000 a day, in just minutes a day, working from home and stuffing mail? If I just click on that link, can I really learn how never to pay taxes again in three simple steps? If I simply call that number, will all of my financial questions be answered so that I can finally protect my wife and kids from the evil that awaits them after I die?

Sometimes when I'm listening to the radio or watching television, I just shake my head. The ads and comments are so outrageous, bordering on preposterous, that I just can't believe the speakers are rational people. Do they believe that stuff themselves? Maybe they aren't rational. Maybe a bunch of raving lunatics have taken over the airwaves and are spitting out any wild statement or claim that comes to mind, hoping to snare enough listeners, watchers, and net surfers to turn a buck.

There are claims for everything... how to be prettier, smarter, skinnier... and then a bunch that I can't mention because I'd be somewhat embarrassed. Let's just say that there are a lot of ads for enhancement that seem questionable at best. But, for whatever reason, this sort of advertising, pitching, and general laziness with the truth seems to be the worst when it comes to money.

We know the claims aren't true; they can't be. If they were, then the person promoting the stuff would be rich beyond imagination and wouldn't need to sell the system/secrets/inside information that they are trying to push onto us!

Still, this sort of thing catches our attention. It eats at us a bit. And I know why. This style, even with all of its nonsense, touches on a weakness we all share: we're fearful of not having enough money. How can we be sure we have enough money to fund the things we want to do and to live the life we want to live? It doesn't matter if we've accumulated $25,000 or $25 million, we still worry.

The problem is that making money is hard, and having it work for you is even harder. There are risks in everything. If you buy CDs, inflation will eat up your returns and then some, leaving you with less than when you started. Taking a chance on stocks is like buying a ticket on a rollercoaster. It could end up okay... or not. Will you get a great ride with some thrills along the way, or end up feeling sick and revisiting that corn dog you had for lunch? It all comes down to the same thing. We do our best to save money and invest it, but nothing on this planet guarantees that our plans will work out.

Nothing.

So we worry. And we read. And sometimes, we fall prey to very seductive messages, which can lead us down the path to a lot of wasted time and even to squandered money.

But our problems with making sense of the overload of information we receive don't stop at the edge of the crazy ads. The mainstream media — because of an agenda or simple ignorance — will take up a cause, which means that most people only get one side of a story.

My goal is to help people make sense of what they hear, see, and read, when it comes to finance. The lines are fuzzy. Money is bound up in the direction of the economy, of course, but it's also closely tied to politics. The Affordable Care Act can cost you money, and taxes will take your money. Both of them matter.

I began writing *Survive & Prosper*, a daily missive, on February 28, 2012, using our Dent Research view of how people live their lives and influence the economy with their personal choices as a backdrop. In that time, the highest tax bracket has increased, the equity markets have surged, bonds have lost value, and the government has mandated that we all buy health insurance. Interestingly, General Motors has become an almost respectable company once again while Detroit has filed for bankruptcy. The recovery keeps getting pushed out a little farther. Students keep taking on more debt. And Americans keep getting older.

It all matters, but some parts of it are more important than others. My goal is to parse the data, explain the relationships, and bring you clear analysis on what these developments mean in general and to you individually.

Having spent more than two decades in the trenches of the world of finance, I have a lot of personal experience on which to draw. I also have degrees in the subject, from what some people consider prestigious universities. Still, that's usually not quite enough to make sense of it all. So I look a little further.

Sometimes I hear my parents in my head, or maybe even a previous boss, imparting wisdom that seems very appropriate. Often, I'm applying life lessons learned on the time-tested battlefields of relationships, like parenthood and marriage. Through it all, I try to keep one question in mind: "Does this make sense?" Unfortunately, the answer is usually a resounding, NO! But often we have to live with it anyway, and it's in our best interest to understand as much as we can as we plan our future.

I hope you will find my explanations and discussions of the topics included here helpful as you go about your own financial journey. Just remember, be wary of the guy who tells you to be thankful for the light at the end of the tunnel… it could be a train.

—Rodney Johnson

CHAPTER 1:
Economy

"It's the economy, Stupid!" was the signature line from Bill Clinton's 1992 presidential campaign. While I think the inclusion of Ross Perot in the contest was more of a deciding factor (he polled 19% of the vote, arguably splitting the conservative vote), there is no question the economy was on people's minds in the early 1990s.

There's no doubt it's on our minds today.

Trying to figure out if the economic skies are blue or if a storm is coming is one of the first things investors and business owners must do. It sets the tone for every decision you make.

This task got complicated after the Great Recession, because, no matter how much the U.S. government and the Fed tried to tell us otherwise, everyday people understood one thing: The economy is still stuck in neutral... at best.

The government doesn't always make the most obvious choice (if ever)...

The current compilation of GDP is ridiculously out of date...

Deflation and inflation have waged war on our economy and our pockets...

It's brutal out there... So here's what you need to know.

—Rodney Johnson

ECONOMICS

A Great Body and a Back End to Die For

October, 2013

A great body and a back-end to die for. Those are the things that grab my attention.

From time to time I'll be driving down the road and my head will turn on a swivel. I'll exclaim something like: "Wow!" or "Look at that!" or even "Awesome!" and my wife will simply smile. She doesn't even have to follow my gaze.

She knows what I'm looking at. It's a car. More specifically, it's a classic car of some sort. I'm a sucker for vintage iron, particularly vehicles from the 1920s and the 1960s.

I'm not nostalgic for them, as I was neither alive in the '20s nor a teen in the '60s, so I'm not trying to relive a prior period of my life.

I just really enjoy the design of these cars. But I don't own one.

Each time I see such a car I think through the mechanical issues associated with keeping one in working order, and the loss of convenience and performance compared to modern cars. The difference between what passed for modern back then and what we have available today is enormous.

Motor Trend Magazine tested three classic cars — a Challenger, Camaro, and Mustang — against their modern day namesakes and the results were clear. The old cars are less comfortable, sloppy in performance, and sluggish in response to everything but the accelerator.

The superiority of the modern vehicles was obvious all the way round. This explains why such cars captivate many people, me included, but why we don't drive them daily. It's simply impractical. When faced with a much better alternative, most everyone will take the obvious choice.

Except the U.S. government...

While no one will ever be nostalgic for a way of measuring economic activity, there's no question that our current compilation of GDP is ridiculously out of date.

This statistic was developed in the late 1920s and early 1930s to measure a very narrow slice of life — production. This time frame included the start of the Great Depression, when business leaders and politicians greatly under-estimated the contraction in the economy, so there was a desperate need for better information.

GDP — estimating the change in business spending, consumer spending, government spending, and exports minus imports — fit the bill and was a great advancement in understanding the economy.

The government would gather information on spending over the course of several months, develop an average, compare it to the prior period, and voila! Suddenly we had a yardstick that we could use to measure the growth or con-traction of economic activity.

Unfortunately, over the last 80 years we've changed woefully little about how we calculate this number.

Yes, the government has tinkered with GDP, adding in a measurement of "rent you could receive if you rented out your home" and other silly things.

Yes, the government makes adjustments for how big of an affect different purchases have on our productivity (new computers add more to the economy than they cost… see if you can figure that one out!).

But in terms of simply measuring numbers, the government waits around for survey results, compiles some averages over an entire calendar quarter, and then revises the number twice over the following two months.

To find out what happened in the first quarter of the year, you have to wait until the last Friday in June for a final, revised number from the U.S. govern-ment.

Haven't they heard of the Internet?

If we can determine iPhone sales in a matter of hours, and Black Friday retail sales within a week, then why does it take three months to develop an average of data from a calendar quarter?

Government hasn't kept up with the times, and yet GDP is one of those numbers that market watchers and politicians hang their hats on.

We can do better.

Right now companies like Premise, which provides real-time information on price changes in 25 cities, are standing at the front of the information line.

There is no reason our hardworking analysts and researchers at the Bureau of Economic Analysis couldn't get in the same line.

We could actually measure real-time numbers from Corporate America, consumers, and the government (where they have to measure their own spending on a lag... really?!) to let us know what is happening today, not 150 days ago.

This would give us much better data to use when making business and investment decisions, and might even aid in monetary and fiscal decisions, if those areas can be helped at all.

As we move to a more real-time measure, we might also drop those idiotic notions that have been bolted on to GDP as time passed, like the owner's-equivalent-rent and hedonic adjustments.

Of course, if we did this, then everyone would get a clear picture of what is going on in the economy... and I'm not sure they'd like it.

Until the government makes such changes, I'm sure it'll keep driving its 1958 Edsel and telling all of us how great it rides.

DEFLATION

The Hallmark of Deflation

November, 2012

We, as homeowners and consumers, are guilty.

For years I've railed against the Bureau of Labor Statistics (BLS) for including the change in home prices, through their convoluted formula, in the Consumer Price Index (CPI).

My point was that, beyond its incomprehensible Owner's Equivalent Rent approach, a change in the value of your home does NOT mean you immediately change your spending, therefore including housing in a measure of short-term inflation is simply wrong.

Think about this in relation to the price of gas…

If your house goes up by 5% this month, beyond popping champagne and dancing a jig, nothing much will change for you. If, however, gasoline goes up by 5%, then chances are you'll feel the pain within a week when you fill up your car.

However, over the long term, housing has a profound effect on the inflation/deflation trend in the economy.

When houses go up in value then the next buyer, the marginal consumer, must pay more. Given that home ownership is still over 60% in the U.S., it is true that most Americans will not be buying a new home tomorrow or even this year. But the rise in prices does materially affect how much new home buyers must spend.

Also, there is the "home-as-an-ATM" factor to consider…

The more equity homeowners had in their homes, the more they could borrow against that home. This led to a wild run up in home equity lines of credit (HELOCs) in the years leading up to 2007/08, which put hundreds of billions of new dollars (funded by debt) into the economy to be spent.

Obviously this funded inflation. After all, this was how consumers continued to ride the buy-everything wave during the 2000s, even though incomes were flat or falling in real terms.

So, when housing prices fall, that creates deflation by removing the ability of homeowners to continually borrow and spend.

Given that what consumers pay for shelter is the largest expense of the household, as prices drop, the next buyer has a lower cost. Obviously, this is great for him, but it is definitely bad for existing owners.

As prices fall, not only are HELOCs harder to get and smaller, but the overall loan-to-value ratio goes up. In short, there is less equity. So the homeowner gets squeezed.

If the value of the home falls below the value of the mortgage, then the homeowner finds himself underwater, working to pay off a loss.

This trend of falling asset prices while debts remain the same is a hallmark of deflation... and we have it in spades in the U.S.

That Leaves Just One More Question...

How does this inflation/deflation play into the long-term finances (like retirement) of the homeowner?

Most people think of retirement savings as their 401k, IRA or some other investment vehicle. This is true of course, but most Americans don't achieve great savings in these vehicles. Instead, most of their savings or accumulated wealth is in their home equity.

In 2010, the Federal Reserve reported that the median drop in financial assets since 2007, for middle income earners, was 40%... from $62,500 to $37,500. That's a big percentage hit.

Meanwhile, the same middle income earner lost 22% of his home value... from $225,000 to $175,000.

Now, the percentage loss on the home doesn't seem as much, but the real dollars lost are more than twice as large.

Which would you rather have? A smaller percentage loss? Or the loss of fewer actual dollars?

Exactly... give me the dollars any day.

At the same time, most investments like stocks and bonds aren't leveraged. So that drop in value from $62,500 to $37,500 was painful, but it was clean. Meanwhile, the same homeowner above had a mortgage of $120,000 in 2007 and a mortgage of $116,000 in 2010. This means the homeowner's equity fell from $105,000 in 2007 to $69,000 in 2010. Ouch.

I'm pretty sure that homeowner was counting on the equity to keep rising, not fall. That means he must now adjust whatever plans he had for the equity. Presumably he'd save more from other sources. Greater savings is the twin of lower consumption, which of course fuels deflation.

For many years we have pointed to a consumer-led deflationary season that would begin around 2008. Our point was that the baby boomers would pass their peak spending years and move into their peak saving years.

The housing boom fueled a credit bubble that allowed this group to spend well beyond their income and other earnings. Now the backside of this credit bubble is here. And bubbles don't deflate gently. They pop.

The Fed has moved mountains to hold off this eventuality, but it can't fight the tide forever. The deflationary forces in our economy today are here to stay for a number of years.

Be prepared.

All Deflation is Not Equal

April, 2013

Anyone who's been to Puerto Rico knows that life on the island moves at a different pace. Even though it is technically a U.S. territory, and it shares many economic traits with us, there's no question that Puerto Rico life simply moves at a slower speed. Many would say this is a feature of the island, not a bug.

Something else not lost on most people is how beautiful the island is. From the historical streets of Old San Juan to the canopy in the rain forest, Puerto Rico is a land rich in beauty…

Yet something in Puerto Rico is not right.

It doesn't matter how pretty it is, or how relaxed its people are, the finances of the island are atrocious. Its bond rating is low. Its deficit is high.

What would happen if the island was forced to right its financial ship immediately?

Well, some things would change.

People would lose jobs as the government cut back dramatically on employment. Retirees would lose some benefits. Islanders would be forced to pay higher taxes, so they'd have less money to spend. All of this would affect businesses on the island, which would see its receipts suffer.

In time — maybe after six months, a year, maybe even two — prices would fall to reflect the lower level of demand.

Some things would *not* change…

The beaches would still be fabulous, for instance. Old San Juan would still be a cool place to have a Mojito. The rain forest would still be one of the best places to hike in the Caribbean.

When you combine these two sets — things that change and things that don't — you come up with an interesting situation that strongly favors one industry… tourism.

Puerto Rico would be an obvious destination for Americans who use the same U.S. dollar as the island, but can now make their dollars go further as prices fall. Yes, there's a pesky language barrier, but people have muddled through that for centuries.

While this scenario is not playing out in Puerto Rico, it IS playing out somewhere else, which is why we should care.

After years of austerity and hand-wringing, the Greek economy is going through deflation. Wages have fallen, jobs have been lost, asset prices have tanked, and retail prices are dropping to reflect the new reality.

But citizens of other countries who use the same currency, like Germany, are not experiencing deflation. Their wages are still strong. So what is the natural decision? To vacation in Greece, of course!

Expect the holiday season in Greece to finally show some life this year*. Not because the Greeks are in a better place, but specifically because they are in a worse place economically, and citizens of other countries are eager to take advantage of it.

Because of the shared currency but individual budget policies, there is a growing disparity between the experiences of citizens in different countries. These differences can, and will, be exploited.

This is one more example of "me-o-centric" economics. It's like rushing to a store that is going out of business, hoping to cash in on a good deal that was brought about by the store's misfortune.

One interesting note is that if there is a significant increase in tourism this season due to lower prices in Greece, then it will actually serve to bolster the local economy and therefore ease some of the Greek pain. In an odd way, the greater their financial misfortune, the more likely they are to attract tourists, and the faster they'll likely recover.

Odd indeed.

* This it did. Greek tourism enjoyed some lift.

Caterpillar Proves Deflation is Alive and Well

May, 2012

I used to love seeing Caterpillar equipment. It made me think of how much fun it would be to drive around on a crane, or excavator, or whatever all those other big machines are called.

Then I got a little older. I still want to drive those machines around, but now I hate to see them. Since I started driving, I associate Caterpillar equipment with road construction and traffic snarls. Whenever I see the familiar black and gold painted earth movers next to the road, I know traffic in that area will be ugly for weeks to come. Ugh.

Now here comes Caterpillar to make one more association for me — and it's deflationary. All because its unionized workers strike… regularly…

Back in February 2009, the equity markets were plunging. Caterpillar was no different. Its stock fell from the mid $80s down to just over $23 per share.

However, the company never reduced its dividend, continuing to pay over $0.40 per share quarterly. And it continued to point out the incredible international demand for its products.

As you might expect, the shares of the company came roaring back, even surpassing its 2008 high, reaching over $110/share.

In Q1 2012, Caterpillar reported $1.6 billion in earnings on $16 billion in revenue. Not too shabby!

So what does the growth of a large company with stable dividends and great earnings have to do with being deflationary? It's all in the wages… or should I say, the U.S. wages…

A Hallmark of Deflation

The workers in the International Association of Machinists and Aerospace Workers Union at the Joliet, IL Caterpillar plant renegotiated their contract. The company wanted to scuttle a pension plan, have more flexibility in hiring temporary workers at greatly reduced wages, have the ability to freeze workers' pay for six years, and require the workers to pay more in health care costs.

Given the company's profitability, its robust earnings, and great sales, you might find it odd that it played hardball when it negotiated with its workers. Why did it do it then? The short answer is: "Because it can."

Labor is an input. It's one of the components that make a company go. When labor is in short supply, meaning there are too few workers to fill the jobs available, wages and benefits go up to attract more people.

The inverse is also true. When labor is plentiful, when there are too many people for the number of jobs available, then wages and benefits fall.

Companies hiring know all too well that there are many more job applicants than there are jobs, so wages remain under pressure. In fact, wages were even falling on an inflation-adjusted basis.

Falling wages are a hallmark of deflation... and we have it in spades.

Take It or Leave It

The interesting point here is that companies adjusted to the economic downturn very quickly. Some companies, like Caterpillar, supply the growth in developing nations like China, so they experience less of a decline.

Part of the economic adjustment in the U.S. was the firing of millions of workers. This allowed companies to match their costs to their sales, thereby returning to profitability rather quickly. But it left the unemployed out in the proverbial cold. So, as new employees are hired, or existing contracts come up for renewal, companies can be very stingy.

The outcome of this situation is long term and it's ugly.

As workers earn less, they can afford less. So consumer spending falls. And tax revenue at the local and national level fails to recover without additional taxes being tacked on.

The end result is that we get a short burst of profits and positive earnings surprises from Corporate America, but eventually the deflationary pressures come back to haunt them. The population and the businesses in a country can't travel different roads for very long.

INFLATION

The Worst of Both Worlds: Inflation vs. Deflation

March, 2013

I was driving by a gas station the other day and realized that regular gas was $3.60/gallon here in Florida. That is about the highest I've ever seen it in February.

It's odd, because I know that not only are Americans driving less, but we're also producing almost two million barrels of oil *more* each day. We use less, produce more, and yet the price of oil sits just under $100/barrel for West Texas Intermediate.

Hmmm.

Things don't get better at the grocery store. Eggs, chicken, beef, coffee… they're all up in price.

I just received my auto insurance renewal. I have two teen drivers, so I understand that my rate is astronomical anyway, but that didn't prepare me for what I saw. My annual premium went from $6,600 to $8,500.

I called and was told that it had nothing to do with the drivers. We all have spotless records. It was entirely due to uninsured motorists.

My daughters' school sent the tuition bill for 2013-2014 and was thrilled to let us know that tuition went up by only — only — 4%.

Say "Hi!" to inflation. You're no doubt already well acquainted. But there's something you need to know about this guy…

He's not the "good" kind of inflation. He's not driven by more people choosing to buy something. Nope, this is a monetary event. The Fed is desperate to create inflation with the intention to motivate spending, hoping it will spur the economy.

It won't.

No matter how much the Fed tries, our main economy is stuck in a deflationary trend, not an inflationary one.

"Deflation?! But you just reminded me about the inflation all around us! What gives?" I hear you ask.

Think of it this way: We have slack demand for goods and services, which leads to falling production and therefore falling employment (high unemployment). This also means we have an overabundance of workers, so income falls.

And money? No one wants it… or at least, fewer people want to borrow it. This means that interest rates are exceptionally low. The Fed is trying to make credit as easy to get as possible, but those who are credit-worthy have no interest. The outcome is interest rates that don't even match the rate of inflation.

That's all pretty deflationary.

Think of what I've just described as the worst of both worlds. We pay higher prices for necessary goods, but we earn less on both our labor and our savings.

The reason we're stuck in this pattern is because the central banks of the world are trying to change the natural cycle of events.

Typically, economies will go through a boom period that is marked by rising consumption, rising prices and rising levels of debt. This cycle becomes self-fulfilling, with most people assuming the good times will go on forever. The idea of risk is thrown out the window.

Of course, it doesn't go on forever. Instead, asset prices come crashing down, demand falls off and all that is left is a bunch of debt. This leads to a conservative period where debt is paid down or written off, demand is weak and money is hard to come by.

We had the risk-on period, now the Fed and other central banks want to erase the whole risk-off period. Unfortunately we can't just wish it away.

The debts are still with us, incomes are down and interest rates almost don't exist. For all the Fed's efforts, what it's really doing is killing our standard of living by draining away what savings and income we have.

You don't have to just sit back and quietly take it. You can fight back. Start by building as many income streams as you can.

HYPERINFLATION

Why We Won't Get Hyperinflation

October, 2012

Years ago, I took the family to Stuttgart, Germany for vacation. One of the stops there is the Mercedes-Benz Museum.

Being very German, the round building is constructed for ease of walking. Visitors take an elevator to the top of the round structure and then walk down a gently sloping path along the outside wall. On the way down, you view successive vintages of vehicles until you reach the bottom, which has the newest — and for sale — models on display. Way cool.

Another cool feature is that, on the wall between floors, there are pictures and trivia from the appropriate time frame.

On the wall between the 1920s and 1930s is a poster illustrating the financial distress of the Weimar Republic...

After WWI, the world hated Germany and demanded war reparations, payable in hard foreign currency. The problem was that the world more or less had a trade embargo on Germany, starving it of access to hard currency. This, along with other ills, led the country to simply print currency with abandon, creating inflation that, at one point, reached 240 million percent.

Many people fear a hyperinflation period will repeat itself in the U.S.

They point to the actions of the Federal Reserve and the debt issuance of the U.S. Treasury as triggers for this pending disaster... If only the world were so simple! It isn't. And we're not 1920s-era Germany. We are a $16 trillion-a-year superpower with a spending addiction, not a cast-out country.

Hyperinflation is NOT in our near future.

Is our penchant for printing money instead of doing the hard work of fiscal reform idiotic? Yep.

Does financial repression steal from our conservative retirees? No doubt.

But are we a nation with declining trade, no international holders of our currency, that is unattractive to foreign buyers? Absolutely not.

We also have that ace-in-the-hole of 5,113 nuclear warheads, per the Department of Defense.

These facts do push the odds in our favor.

The U.S. is the largest economy on the planet and is among the richest. Even though we have done our best to repel foreign investors through Sarbanes-Oxley, the new Consumer Financial Protection Bureau, and the IRS, foreign capital still flows in. In short, we are attractive in spite of how badly we treat others.

When we add to this the fact that our currency and our debt is widespread in the world, the chances of large holders spurning our currency is remote.

The reason is that currency has to be exchanged for something else. In a world marked by a race to the bottom, where everyone wants the cheapest currency so their exports are least expensive, there's not a government in sight that wants their currency to be the "go-to" in this situation.

If another currency displaces the U.S. dollar as the currency of reserve, then that currency will shoot up in value, harming exports and ruining trade balances.

As Switzerland found out in the summer of 2011, when everyone rushes into your currency it makes your exports prohibitively expensive and your assets all but untouchable to the rest of the world. That's bad.

Then there's the little thing of power and reach…

The conversation about economics tends to revolve around currency valuations, trade, the psychology of markets and government intervention. What people often dismiss is security. This is probably because right now world security is not in question. No one anticipates a world war or outbreak of conflict between very large powers. And that's because there is only one very large military power today… us.

The good ol' U.S. of A.

We exert influence in countless areas, not because of the U.S. dollar, but because of the U.S. military. The very basic question is: "Do you want to be aligned with us or against?" If you are with us, you won't take actions that debase our currency. Leave that to the professionals at the Fed.

Our view?

The dollar won't crumble into utterly useless pieces of ink-soaked cotton just yet… hyperinflation is the gold bugs' pipe dream.

We say hoard dollars.

In times like these, they're going to gain value.

Good Stories Built on Terrible Logic

May, 2013

We are all bad drivers near our homes... at least that's how the story goes.

Statistically speaking, 80% of all accidents occur within two miles of the home, and it's the driver's fault. Obviously, we all become blind, inattentive drivers as we near our own driveways.

We know the streets so well and we're so familiar with landmarks that we fail to take basic precautions. We speed. We ignore stop signs. We start thinking about what's for dinner, what new hole the dog dug, which little projects we can get done around the house before our favorite TV show starts.

It's the old adage: familiarity breeds contempt.

The problem is, this theory and its proof may sound reasonable when you consider just one piece of the puzzle... but when you start looking at other pieces, suddenly, this picture is all wrong.

That statistic of 80% is only part of the story...

It turns out that people do 90% of their driving within two miles of their homes. If only 80% of accidents are within that distance, then drivers are actually safer when closer to home.

With this additional information we can spin an entirely different story...

We pay *more* attention when we get closer to home because our kids are in the neighborhood. We know the landmarks so well that we recognize when something is out of place.

It's amazing what we can rationalize when given just one simple piece of information. And how adding a new piece of information can take us in a whole different direction.

Take retail sales for instance.

The level of retail sales is at an all-time high. This is true.

The level of retail sales adjusted for inflation (called real retail sales) is also at an all-time high, having recently surpassed the 2007 high.

Using this information, pundits now claim we're well on the long path to recovery.

This might seem obvious. If retail sales have improved that means consumers are driving the economy higher. If there was some sort of long-term decline occurring, wouldn't this figure be decreasing?

Hmmm.

This sure sounds good, but it's missing an important detail. It's missing a measurement of the number of people involved.

While it's true that the absolute dollar figure of sales has increased, it's also true that the number of people in our economy has increased. When we account for the number of people by measuring real retail sales on a per capita basis, then the retail sales number has actually fallen.

It's like measuring sales in a store, where the goal is to make sure that each customer spends more. If revenue is increasing, say from $1 million to $1.1 million (up 10%), then things look pretty good. But if the number of people shopping has increased from 30,000 to 40,000 (up 33%), then the spending per customer has actually fallen.

If I own a store where revenue is increasing, this might not be a problem. However, if my costs go up with every new client because my business is customer service driven, then this can lead to a drop in profits. It is the same with the U.S. economy.

A rise in retail sales is good, but if the sales per person is falling, then, on average, each of us has less.

And this is exactly where we are today.

But this might not be such a bad thing… Perhaps part of the reason real retail sales per capita aren't reaching old highs is because consumers have chosen to lower credit card purchases.

Are these tied together? Maybe. Or maybe this has occurred because consumers don't have as much average income, given the fall in real wages.

Either way, it's a story of "less," and one that is becoming common during this economic winter season.

The War Between Government Statistics and Reality

December, 2013

There's a war going on, but it has no human casualties and gets little attention. There are no guns and no blood. Yet this war gets a lot of press.

This war is the struggle between inflation and deflation.

So far there are only a few winners... and an awful lot of losers.

On November 15, 2013, the Bureau of Labor Statistics (BLS) released inflation numbers, showing that the Consumer Price Index had fallen by 0.1% for the month of October and had risen by only 1% for the year.

Typically you'd think this is great news. After all, low inflation means our dollars are holding their value, right?

Instead, economists and Fed members are worried that we're at risk of falling into deflation. They worry that if prices start to drop, spenders will hold back as they wait for further price reductions, thereby pushing the economy back into recession.

It's called the paradox of thrift...

Saving money causes a falling economy, which hurts the very savers (through job losses and falling asset values) that started the whole thing!

To fight this possible deflation, the Fed and other central banks print money like crazy. But their actions aren't causing widespread gains in wages or inducing higher spending, although they are causing asset prices like stocks to shoot higher. This has allowed the gains of their actions to be concentrated in a few hands while everyone else gets to plod their way through life with flat or falling earnings and zero return on their savings.

The problem is that the Fed and others want to turn the economic tide, somehow beating or changing a business cycle that has existed as long as people have worked with specialized labor and used debt.

I've got news for them.

We *are* in deflation. Consumers want less debt and are refusing to rack up more on credit cards. This is the very natural and healthy response to years of spending on credit.

We should welcome this trend... even encourage it. The faster we work our way through the deflation of credit reduction the faster we can move on.

But the members of the Fed aren't buying it. They don't want anyone to claim they "allowed" deflation on their watch, as if they have the almighty power to make consumers do what they want.

So they hold down interest rates, punishing us with negative savings rates, and work to bolster inflation so that we pay more for goods and services… brilliant!

I have a message for members of the Fed and other central banks:

Please. Stop already.

We don't want to spend more… and no matter what CPI tells you, even though prices have fallen for gadgets and widgets, we do have higher prices in some key areas of life. All you have to do is ask us about it.

Been to the grocery store? You've paid more.

Written a tuition check? Prices are higher.

Bought medicine or paid an insurance premium? Welcome to higher costs.

In daily life, we're taking it in the shorts.

In one area — gasoline — prices dropped fairly dramatically over the last year (down 10%), but this is from already high prices. Think about it, gas is over $3 per gallon! That's huge.

Just because some government statistic shows modest price movements doesn't mean that things are rosy on Main Street.

The really sad part about CPI not capturing what happens in daily life is that the numbers to do so are readily available. The U.S. government already captures data on how we spend and how prices actually change… it's just not reported in a useable way.

I don't think there's a conspiracy to hide such information, just a constant effort to make our economy look better than it really is. After all, who wants to take responsibility for making it more expensive to live while wages fall?

I'm sure that neither Ben Bernanke nor Janet Yellen want to be remembered as "The Killer of Our Standard of Living."

So next time you read a government statistic about inflation, don't take it too seriously. Instead, turn to us. We'll give you the real numbers. And then we'll tell you what you can do about it.

The Dent Index vs. the CPI

February, 2014

There's an old joke about a hot air balloonist who gets lost.

He brings the balloon near to the ground and yells out to the first person he sees: "Excuse me! Can you tell me where I am?"

The man on the ground says: "Sure! You are approximately 30 feet above ground at 39.04 degrees North by 98.15 degrees West!"

The balloonist replies: "You must be an engineer. You gave me the exact information I asked for, and yet I still have no idea where I am."

The man on the ground responds: "You must be a lawyer. You're lost and asked me for help, which I've provided, and yet somehow you now blame me for your predicament."

This joke comes to mind whenever the U.S. government releases statistics.

I'd like to know how the economy is doing but I don't find their information useful at all. While I didn't get lost in a hot air balloon, I'm still baffled long after the reports have been made public. Clearly, government statistics need better reporting, so that's exactly what we've done, and we've started with inflation.

When calculating its Consumer Price Index (CPI), the Bureau of Labor Statistics (BLS) compiles prices on thousands of items every month and then compares them with the prices of those same goods and services for the previous month.

On the face of it, this sounds pretty good. Unfortunately, digging into the details reveals problems…

The BLS includes housing in its calculation of inflation. That seems right. After all, we all live somewhere. But does the price of housing actually change for most people, month to month?

Of course it doesn't, because almost two-thirds of people own their homes. Unless they have an adjustable rate mortgage, their cost of housing doesn't change at all. Among the remaining people, many have long-term leases on apartments or condos. That means the percentage of people who experience a change in the price of housing during the year is quite small. Yet this component represents more than 30% of the CPI, simply because it's a big piece of most family budgets.

Then there's the idea that one measure of CPI applies to everyone. Do you buy the same goods and services as your kids or parents? Or more to the point, do you spend the same amount of your monthly budget on the same items as other age groups?

Of course you don't. Young people tend to spend a lot more money on education expenses, while older Americans spend significantly more on pharmaceuticals. So a dramatic rise in the cost of education would affect younger Americans much more than it would affect everyone else, especially older Americans. Yet the BLS treats the change in the cost of these goods and services — along with everything else — as if they affect all people the same way. It doesn't make sense.

To address this, we've developed our own Dent Age-Targeted Inflation Indices to capture how different age groups spend money, and therefore, how inflation in different segments of the economy affects each group.

We start by stripping out housing, so that consumers can see how they're actually being affected by things that fluctuate in price, like food, gasoline, heating oil, household goods, etc.

The official inflation numbers for January 2014 showed the 12-month rate at 1.56%. Our calculation of inflation for 18 to 24 year olds was a little less than that, at 1.17%, while young families got a bigger break, with inflation running at 1.06%. The 65 and over group had the biggest jump in prices, at 1.32%.

While we're in a period of deflation — as we are now — the changes in each group, or even the difference between the official rate and the inflation different age-groups experience, can be small. However, when inflation does come back, it won't be evenly spread across all categories.

Just look back at the 2000s…

In the CPI basket, from 2000 through January 2014, energy surged higher by 114%, while education costs moved up by 106%. Medical costs increased by "only" 67%. Meanwhile, the overall inflation number plodded higher by only 39%, which is really close to the move higher for housing at 38%.

Clearly, a 106% move higher in education has a dramatic effect on young people, while an almost 70% increase in medical costs hits our aging population. The 100%+ move in energy smacks everyone.

As we move through the rest of the Economic Winter Season* and then into Spring, we'll keep track of these numbers and let you know when they're getting too far afield from the official releases. That way you can have the right set of facts, and useful information to boot!

* At Dent Research we monitor an 80-year economic cycle that has four seasons. 2008 was the beginning of the fourth and final season of the cycle which runs through 2023.

INTEREST RATES

Life on the Rollercoaster

July, 2013

In Houston, Texas there was once an amusement park called Astroworld, near the Astrodome. It boasted a very tall, wooden rollercoaster known as the Texas Cyclone. Of course this coaster had many cars, but only two mattered — the front and the back.

To sit at the front was to have an unobstructed view of Houston as the coaster clinked its way to the top of the first hill and prepared for the first heart-stopping drop. As the cars began to cascade over the drop, the first car was literally pushed faster down the hill, giving you that rush of adrenaline. It was way cool.

The back of the coaster was a different story.

The view wasn't very good — lots of other people's hands in the air — and of course you never arrived first. But you did have a unique experience…

…that of whiplash.

The occupants of the last seat got the rush of being thrown from side to side as the little coaster train rounded corners at top speed. After the first few cars had been pushed around a corner, the last car was almost ripped around the corner as it was pulled along.

At 12-years old, what a rush! Now that I'm nearing 50, I'm not so keen on the last seat on a rollercoaster. Yet that's where I find myself, along with everyone else who deals with interest rates.

In the summer of 2013 the Fed created a mighty storm in fixed income, causing rates to shoot to the moon before falling back a bit. Its transgression was hinting that its bond buying program would soon be reduced. It threw the markets into disarray.

The question people had to ask was: Where do rates go from here?

To ponder this question is to think about two different dimensions at the same time.

There is the economic health of the country, which should inform the Fed about if and when to back off of its bond buying…

And then there's the possible unwinding of the yield compression in different types of bonds.

Both dimensions are important.

It appears that, as we expected and have discussed, the Fed's comments about tapering were premature. It didn't slow bond buying until much later in the year. It spent a lot of energy telling everyone that they were missing the point.

Yes, the Fed will back off of bonds, but no, it won't be today... and it won't be until the economy shows significant strength.

I don't see that happening anytime soon, which means it's more likely that Treasury bonds and extraordinarily high quality bonds will actually see their interest rates fall in the months ahead.

This is particularly true of short-term interest rates.

When investors around the world get skittish they turn to U.S. Treasuries, but not all maturities are created equal. People looking to simply preserve purchasing power don't take maturity risk. They stay close, which means a possible increase in demand for short-term Treasuries in the case of an economic scare (like a southern European country having a crisis, for instance) causing a drop in yields and a bump in price.

This is very different from the outlook for high yield bonds and emerging market bonds. While the past several years have been good for these sorts of investments, it looks like the bloom is off the rose.

Apparently, people who simply bought such things because they offered more interest now realize the increase in interest comes with an increase in risk. If the U.S. economy and/or the world economy experience a further decline, expect these types of bonds to fall in price as demand drops off, causing their interest rates to rise.

Either way it appears that the days of exceptionally cheap mortgage money and auto loan money are over. The rates are still low today, but the chances of seeing sub-4% on a mortgage again are slim.

If you're in the market for bonds, do your due diligence. While there's risk... there are many opportunities.

For those willing to do their homework, there are many bonds that have been battered at the back of the rollercoaster and now offer a decent yield. Just don't be cajoled into buying junk.

ENTITLEMENTS

Entitled to Something From an Entitlement Program?

November, 2012

To be entitled is to have the legal right or just claim to something. And when we talk about entitlements from the U.S. government, we're usually talking about money.

Social Security is an entitlement program, as is Medicare. In this sense, recipients have a legal right to receive benefits from these programs because that is how the law is written.

But what everyone knows is that these programs contain... nothing.

If these programs hold a big bucket of air, then what exactly are recipients entitled to? As it turns out, they're entitled to a share of the productive ability of current workers.

Because of the way we fund these programs, the law states that retirees get a share of each worker's paycheck. And that's what causes the problem...

For obvious reasons entitlement programs do not expand and contract, or at least not too much. There are cost of living adjustments in Social Security benefits and the government is always trying to trim around the edges of benefits by taxing them or changing enrollment requirements.

But every change to what people receive requires a change in the law. For Social Security, there is a huge, growing amount of benefits to which recipients have a legal claim. For Medicare, there is a bigger, but unknown pool of benefits to which recipients have a legal claim.

As we all know, the unknown part of Medicare is how much bigger will the liability be, not whether it will shrink. Now compare these known and growing payments with the flip side, meaning how they are funded.

We take from workers and their employers 12.4% of their first $110,000 for Social Security. Medicare charges 2.9% on all W-2 income. This 15.3% is a steady percentage, no question, but the payroll itself is not.

What happens when our economy goes through a tremendous setback and millions of people lose their jobs? Obviously 15.3% of nothing is nothing, so these people are not contributing as long as they are unemployed. And when they return to the workforce with a lower salary? They are contributing less.

What happens when there are fewer workers in the workforce? Well, the percentage of 15.3% remains, but just like the example above it is charged on fewer people.

Of course the big question is: "What happens when both of these things occur?"

Well, this is where we are today. There are fewer people working, as noted by the falling labor force participation rate. And earnings have fallen. This leads to the entitlement program funding mechanism (the tax) bringing in less revenue. But the recipients are still entitled to their benefits. So the programs go bankrupt faster.

Then what happens?

This is what we as a society have to decide.

There are many ways to go at entitlements. None of them give a feel-good answer.

There has to be a ranking of priorities and some sort of grand compromise. We can raise taxes (taking more of every worker's earnings), we can lower benefits, or do some combination.

What we *cannot* afford to do is stick our heads in the sand and ignore this for another year, or two, or ten.

With 80 million boomers on the edge of retirement, the sooner we make informed, affordable decisions, the sooner everyone finds out the long-term rules of the game.

Until then, we'll simply have to keep guessing as to what, exactly, people are entitled to.

Your (Non) Share of Entitlement Programs

May, 2012

Medicare is broke and broken.

President Johnson introduced the program in the 1960s as part of his "Great Society." He didn't originate the idea of health care for the elderly, but he was the President that eventually got it passed.

The original scope of the program was to provide affordable care — not free care — to Social Security recipients. Initially the program was a success. It did indeed provide health care to those who otherwise could not afford it. Then, of course, time and Congress took their toll.

Time took its toll by revealing that health care costs would soon outstrip the inflation rate of most every other item, including general prices, wages and interest rates.

Congress took its toll by ever-widening who qualified to receive Medicare coverage, and then failing to stick with cost-reducing measures needed to keep Medicare from spiraling out of control.

What we're left with today is a program that covers tens of millions of people, at a cost to the participants far short of the cost of the care. The bottom line is: Medicare brings in less than it spends right now.

But Congress didn't stop there...

Every year Congress passes temporary laws that stop automatic cuts in Medicare payments. One such cut is a required reduction in the fees paid to doctors. This mandatory cut is part of a law from over a decade ago, created with the intention of helping keep Medicare solvent.

The idea was, if Medicare began spending more than it received in revenue (tax payments), then doctors were supposed to have their reimbursement fees cut by 5%.

Of course, that never happened.

Medicare has been underwater since 2008. So, for the five years since then, including 2008, doctors should have seen a reduction in their pay. By now, the drop would have been over 25%.

But, every year, Congress has passed what is called the "doctor's fix," to put off this cut. Once again, in January 2013 there was supposed to be a mandatory cut of doctor's fees, and now the number is up to 31%. Will it happen? Not a chance. In fact, Congress is working to permanently unwind this automatic cut so that it can avoid the issue altogether.

Instead, we'll go along pretending that all is well... that the U.S. treasury bonds in the Medicare Trust Fund are really worth something... that the program really can save money by enacting fictitious cuts somewhere in the future... that everyone will have health care in whatever form or amount they want.

At least, some people will keep pretending this to be the case. For the rest of us, reality keeps getting a bit uglier.

It's not enough that Medicare has lost money every year since 2008.

It's not enough that Congress can't find the political will to simply stick with existing methods of bringing down costs, much less work on new ways to reign in the runaway spending.

Additionally, we have over 60 million baby boomers that will be retiring in the next 12 to 15 years, all looking for their piece of the Medicare pie. This is what should scare you.

There will be adjustments made. And adjustments never work for two groups — taxpayers and those with assets. If you are in either one of these categories, be warned. Medicare will be balanced on your back, no matter how much it hurts.

CENTRAL BANKS

Give Me My Money Back... You Thief!

January, 2013

$88.9 billion.

That's how much "profit" the Federal Reserve sent to the U.S. Treasury in 2012 to spend "any way it likes."

Of course, this is profit from theft, which is usually punishable in the U.S.

Here's how it works...

The Fed prints money out of thin air, buys interest paying securities, gathers up all the interest (less expenses), calls it "profit," and sends it on to the U.S. Treasury.

Only, when the Fed prints money it's stealing from everyone who is a net saver, which obviously doesn't include the U.S. government. So why then do we allow the Fed to steal from all of us, only to reward the biggest debtor in the country?

I've got a better plan... give the money back!

There are roughly 202 million adults in the U.S. At $88.9 billion the Fed could send every adult $440. They stole it from us, why not return it?

Ok, there are a few small reasons this won't work...

It turns out that not every adult is a net saver, particularly the young adults who are just starting their careers. So sending $440 back to them would not equitably reimburse those who were harmed by the original theft.

Then there's the problem of actually getting $440 to 202 million Americans. That's no small task.

There is a more elegant solution. Destroy it.

Oh... wait. We can't.

For whatever reason, we have set up our system so that we can't destroy any funds the Fed created out of thin air. We've made this inflationary process a permanent, one-way move.

Why? What sense does it make?

If the Fed is serious about its role as the keeper of our currency, then it should follow a very conservative path.

It wants to buy mortgage-backed securities to keep mortgage rates low. I don't agree with it, but I get it.

It wants to buy U.S. Treasuries to keep overall interest rates low, as well as drive investors into risky assets. Again, I disagree, but I get it.

However, there is NO point served by sending our dysfunctional U.S. Treasury even more money to spend... money that was not openly taxed away through clear debate and policy, but was rather taken by force from an un-elected committee.

Instead of sending the monies to the U.S. Treasury, the Federal Reserve should perform a reverse transaction every time it receives interest. It should zero out all funds except what is needed to perform its duties.

This is possible because the Fed has the only magic keyboard in the U.S. that allows for the creation... and therefore destruction... of money through one-sided transactions.

Think $88.9 billion is a small number?

Consider that right now the Fed is printing $85 billion every single month. The size of the payments to the U.S. Treasury over the next several years will only get bigger.

And every week the Fed continues to steal from you and me, and make payments to the U.S. Treasury.

I'd like my money back... or at least my purchasing power.

The Fed Flashes an L-Shaped Hand Sign to Savers, Workers and Retirees

January, 2013

I try to stay away from teen-speak. But with three teenagers, I'm constantly hit with terms I didn't learn in school. I hear things like "bromance" in conversation or read "ROFLMAO" in a text message… I even see the latest in hand signals like the thumb and forefinger in the shape of an "L" on the forehead.

I now know the meaning of each of the examples above, but keeping up with it all is tiring. Plus my kids laugh at me when I try to use such things in conversation.

Still, it's proved useful outside of the teen world…

As it turns out, the Fed has been flashing the typical American the "loser" sign for some time now. And while I don't feel I'm missing much by not keeping up with teen-speak, I'm definitely missing a lot, including money from my wallet, thanks to the Fed.

For the last five years the Fed has used unconventional tactics to attack what it sees as "major issues" in the U.S. financial system. From bailouts to loans to straight up money printing, the Fed has been moving mountains (of cash) to get things done.

In short, it's trying to turn the tide of deflation that comes from debt reduction by cranking up the printing presses to full speed. This action is supposed to create inflation, and it does to a degree…

The Fed wants inflation and wants it badly.

The Fed wants stuff to cost more.

It needs prices to move higher so people will be compelled to buy stuff before it gets out of their reach. From cars, to homes, to gadgets, the Fed is desperate to make sure we face the prospect of having to pay more so we make the decisions to rather pay sooner!

This is supposed to boost demand, which will, in theory, boost production… thereby leading to increased employment and voila! The economy is "fixed!"

Sort of.

There's just one problem. It doesn't really work that way.

The Fed has definitely made prices go higher in some areas. Look at health care, or education, or food, or energy.

The Fed's efforts have even mitigated some of the fall in the housing market, although the bubble that burst was so big that prices still fell 30% to 40% (and probably have more to go).

What the Fed has NOT done, and could not do, is somehow make incomes go up. Or, for that matter, make it so that consumers don't have to save for their retirement so they can rather spend their money now on things like their children's education.

This means the average American has flat income but rising costs (as prices go up around him). The net result: a falling standard of living.

That's right. A big "L" for loser.

So, who are the "winners?"

That would be large banks, who not only got bailed out, but now benefit from the very real idea that if any trouble comes their way they'll simply get bailed out again. The banks also get to make loans at 4% to 5% while paying depositors between nothing and 0.5%.

What a gift!

Equity traders and investment banks are loving this new normal, where funds and bank trading operations reach out on the risk scale to buy more and more, driving markets and prices higher.

Along the way there are a few scraps that fall from the table…

If we have retirement accounts with some equity exposure, chances are we have seen some growth. Of course, this has been more than offset by the loss of income on conservative fixed income, but let's not quibble.

All of this highlights the ugly truth about inflation: it's not equal… it's not fair.

Inflation spreads through an economy unevenly, bringing unearned benefits to some and undeserved pain to others. Government officials get to run deficits with exceptionally low interest rates, bad-faith bankers get to keep their jobs and earn millions in profits, while consumers are put on the hook for higher public debt while their incomes fall further behind the cost of living.

This is what happens with monetary (money printing) inflation... and it must be so. If all things remained equal, if there was no shift in wealth, no change in value that took place, then why would any central bank ever print money!?

There must be an effect they are looking for. And I'm here to tell you that there is... and it has been accomplished.

What is being taken from us is being given to others.

FED TAPER

When is $10 Billion NOT a Big Number?

December, 2013

There's an old joke about how to become a millionaire. Start with $2 million and then lose $1 million. The joke is all about perspective, which is exactly what's required when considering the Fed's actions on December 18, 2013.

It's like a thief who comes by every night and takes $10 out of your wallet. You know who it is, and you know how he operates, but you can't stop him.

Finally, he tells you that he might stop. That's good news! You get excited.

Then he tells you that instead of taking $10 every night, he'll only take $9.

Suddenly, you don't feel so good. But that's OK, because the thief wasn't keeping the money. He was distributing it to a bunch of other people. They were quite worried that the thief would slow down the money train. So when he told everyone he would simply steal a little less, well, the recipients were pretty excited.

That about sums up the taper… and explains why the markets were so thrilled with the initial reaction yesterday.

The end result is that the Fed is going to (ever so gently) slow down its bond buying, which is not fueling an economic recovery, but is crushing savers.

This should lead to higher interest rates down the road, but not today. It all depends on how quickly the Fed slows its bond buying.

Keep in mind that the Fed is on track to buy the equivalent of almost 80% of the bonds the U.S. Treasury issued this year. That doesn't leave a lot of inventory for other people to pick from, so long-term interest rates should remain low, or edge up only slightly as 2014 progresses.

If the Fed changes its rate of bond purchases, then interest rates will respond (buying fewer bonds should push rates higher).

But this doesn't even touch the real topic at hand. That is, short-term interest rates. This is where Wall Street makes money.

The Fed announced that short-term interest rates will remain zero-bound for an "extended" period of time. This means beyond the estimate of 2015.

Our view — which I've written on several occasions — is that short-term interest rates will remain exceptionally low into 2017. This means the interest rate on which margin rates and portfolio margin rates are set will remain exceptionally low for years.

So all of those investment funds and investment banks that use leverage (borrowing against assets to buy even more assets) can continue using cheap debt to fuel their returns. What a gift!

Of course, it doesn't work out for everyone.

Gold buyers got another black eye when gold fell out of bed and sank below $1,200 an ounce because the Fed wasn't seen as stoking inflation. Really, these guys are in for more beatings as we expect gold to fall well below $1,000 an ounce.

The modest drop in bond buying is being viewed as a prop to the U.S. dollar, given that the Japanese will have to print more yen, while the euro is at its recent highs even though the euro zone is languishing. Dollar strength equals gold weakness. That's gotta hurt a little.

Unfortunately the full scope of the Fed announcement was that Wall Street will continue to rake in bucks, savers won't get much relief, and those preparing for a death blow to the U.S. dollar took another hit.

How the Chinese Government Created a Problem for Us

January, 2013

In China there's an old parable about an eight-year old son in a poor family who wants his parents to sleep well…

Given the time of year, there was the constant buzz of mosquitoes in the air, the all-too-familiar bites and slapping as the hungry bloodsuckers landed for their feast, but the family couldn't afford mosquito netting. So to assist his parents, the boy sat shirtless all night, trying to draw the mosquitoes to his bare skin so his parents could rest easier.

One day the father awoke before the son could put his shirt back on. He saw the welts and knew what had happened.

The story spread through the village and was eventually reported to the authorities, who were so impressed by the boy's devotion they granted him a scholarship to the academy. They also gave the family mosquito netting.

This story is one of 24 Filial Exemplars in China. They're like our own Grimm Fairy Tales. In each Exemplar, the children sacrifice for members of the older generations.

The reason I'm telling you about them is because the Chinese government recently updated these 24 stories… It replaced displays of devotion by drawing mosquitoes away with suggestions to take your aging parents on vacation, or buy them health insurance.

The government didn't go down this path because it wants to encourage family unity. It did it for more selfish — a.k.a. survival — reasons.

Without the support of the children, the Chinese government cannot possibly support the parents. The numbers are simply overwhelming…

In 1982 there were 85 million Chinese people over the age of 60 (5% of the population). At the same time, there were 342 million kids under the age of 14 (33% of the population).

In 2010 the number of 60-plus-year-olds had grown to 85 million, or 8.8% of the population, while the number of children had fallen to 222 million, or 17% of the population.

This was all on purpose. The Chinese One-Child Policy is well known, and it worked. The economy was able to shoot higher, fed by a huge generation of workers (15-64 year-olds), without the economic drag of children.

But now the dark side of this policy is coming back to haunt the Chinese. Not only are there many fewer children to support aging parents, but those children have often moved hundreds of miles away to pursue work. The aging population in China is largely on its own, and the government has scant resources to help them.

In a time of slowing economies around the world, China has kept its economic engine on track by fueling internal growth through capital spending.

As exports have slowed due to falling demand in the euro zone, the U.S., and elsewhere, the Chinese government has continued funding internal projects. The nation has built thousands of miles of roads, numerous dams, power plants and skyscrapers. While the natural forces turning the wheels of progress are in play, they are certainly getting a very large helping hand from the government.

This has left little in terms of resources to be set aside for the growing demands of the elderly in the years to come. The national health care system in China has recently been revamped, but it isn't generous... and is arguably insufficient.

As for national retirement, the funding is laughable because local politicians have raided the coffers. This leaves the ever-dwindling ranks of children on the hook to care for their parents, no matter how far away they are.

This connection became even stronger — in a legal sense — when the Chinese government made it possible for aging parents to sue their children for better care.

The problem is the rest of the world isn't simply a spectator to this fight. The Chinese economy consumes large amounts of natural resources purchased around the world as it builds products for export and engages in local capital spending.

At the same time, much has been made about the explosion in spending that will happen when Chinese middle class consumers break open their piggy banks and start chasing the Western dream of ever-rising consumption.

What if both of these trends hit the brick wall of demographics?

What if much of the resources currently earmarked for internal expansion to keep the factories humming and workers whistling have to be devoted to caring for the elderly?

What if the saved resources of middle class families have to be spent on a nursing home for Grandpa instead of another car?

Yes, these types of spending do still feed the economy, but not in the same way. While supporting an aging group that is expected to top quarter of a billion people by 2050 is morally and philosophically correct, it doesn't lead to an increase in the tools of production or greater exports.

It can lead to a global slowdown in commodity markets as the great Chinese machine shifts to a lower gear. This would reverberate around the globe, hitting Australia first, then branching out to the Pacific Rim nations and finally reaching Latin America.

The Chinese miracle economy was no miracle. In some ways — like the One-Child Policy — it was a choice. In other ways it was happenstance — opening their economy coincided with a debt-fueled consumption boom in the West.

Regardless, the phenomenal growth can no longer resist the law of gravity. The laborers unencumbered by children gave the country an advantage for many years. Now they have to be given care and comfort.

And in some way, we're all going to pay for it.

CHAPTER 2:
Investing

Investing should not be like a box of chocolates. We should not be surprised by what happens. Instead, it should be deliberate, with purpose, and with a plan. If an investment seems too good to be true, it is. One pill won't make you skinny, and typically one stock won't make you rich. If any security can go up that fast, it can buy a ticket for the ride down as well. But there are so many investments to choose from, it's hard to understand all the varieties, much less which ones make sense. Unfortunately, even some of the old stodgy ones, like municipal bonds and CDs, need to be reviewed sometimes.

That's what you'll read in this section: writings that remove the surprise… that show you what plans could work best… what you should be wary of and what you should jump into… what you need to know to understand the world of investing.

This section also contains a topic that can make people crazy… the value of the U.S. dollar. If this is a hot button for you, then please pay special attention! My view is far from the norm, and can save you a lot of money by keeping you from buying the wrong things!

—Rodney Johnson

Small Cap and Large Cap Investments Aren't Enough

October, 2012

I wrote yesterday about the current markets being much more like Vegas than any reasoned approach to analysis. Market participants, professional and amateur alike watch their screens on government-announcement days to see what sort of fresh incentive will be offered. Then they spend the next hour or two trying to figure out if it's good or bad.

That's no way to restore confidence in our financial markets, but given that we all hold financial assets we are forced to be in the game.

However, we are free to choose how we participate. We can watch out for pitfalls and strategically avoid them when we see them ahead. And we can grab opportunities that come into play.

In this Economic Winter Season, it is vital to think outside boxes… in particular, the Morningstar box.

Morningstar always made me smile. The company grew to fame by creating a nine-box matrix that neatly categorized equity investments from growth to value and then small cap to large cap.

Once the boxes were fixed, the race was on to "balance" one's investments among the different styles listed.

This led money managers to focus solely on one area… to the point where they became known as a "large cap value man" or a "small cap blend manager."

My smile was brought on by the thought of what these guys do when their particular type of investment fell out of favor. While a guy might be riding high on mid-cap growth stocks, when the tide turns and these stocks get hammered, his best bet is to shift into whatever is favored next. Unfortunately, many of these managers are bound by their prospectuses to remain in a certain area of investing.

Don't fall into this trap.

Style Has No Place Here

One of the keys to success in the current environment is recognizing that style has no place here. There is no distinguishing between large cap growth and small cap blend. The only thing that matters at the moment is "risk on" and "risk off."

The difference is a determination as to whether global sentiment believes we will all be saved by central banks and that inflation among risk assets is a gift... or that nothing can save us now, all currencies will die and we should hunker down for the great implosion.

This manic depressive market view drives everything. And it seems to change about once a quarter.

Knowing this allows investors to take a step back, turn off the TV, put down the paper and ask a few questions.

When the world is "risk off," what might do well? Income investments come to mind.

When the world is "risk on," what's the best choice? Commodities are a start.

From this simple starting point investors can build a short list of "risk on" and "risk off" investments that they choose to hold either as a group, knowing they will participate in both phases but also give a little back, or they can choose to move back and forth with the rhythm of the investment world.

Whichever you choose, make sure to stay out of the boxes.

Save Yourself From Hedge Funds

July, 2013

Consider this a warning.

The SEC (Securities and Exchange Commission) is relaxing the rules on how hedge funds can market.

It's a mistake because it means you'll be bombarded with advertisements from these entities. The ads will be slick. They'll be enticing. They'll tout returns that most people can only dream of.

And your job is to turn away.

Take a page from Homer's Odyssey… Odysseus had his crew tie him to the mast so he wouldn't be able to steer towards the Sirens and shipwreck on the rocks.

Okay, maybe you don't need to be tied down, but definitely turn the page, change the channel or do anything else to stay away from these funds! They can be destructive to your wealth.

A short (true) story on how messed up things can become will show why most people have no business in such investments.

In 1999 there was a hedge fund that rode the Internet craze to dizzying heights. The fund was up 332% in that one year alone… and up another 53% in the first couple of months of 2000. Then the wheels came off.

By the middle of April 2000, the fund was down 89% for that year. Think about what would have happened if you were an investor in that fund.

You put in $100,000 on January 1, 1999. By the end of the year your account showed $432,000, at which point you owed the manager his fee, 2% of the account value for management plus 20% of the profits. That equates to $75,000. Still, you have $357,000 left, which is a 257% gain. Not too shabby.

But by early April the fund has fallen 89% for the year, bringing your account down to $39,270 (89% of the ending 1999 balance of $357,000). That's awful… but it gets worse.

You see, this is a hedge fund, so it's a partnership. As a partner, you're distributed paper profits every year, even if you don't take them out of your account.

Because this was a short-term trading fund, let's assume you were allocated all the profits in your account at the end of 1999… so $257,000. Your tax bill at the 35% rate would be about $90,000. Unfortunately, your account is now only worth $39,270. So your hedge fund investment went from $100,000 to $39,270, to… a negative $50,730. Ouch!

Don't get me wrong, there is nothing inherently wrong with hedge funds. The problem is that few investors actually understand how they work, so when they invest in them it's like they're jumping into a very dark pool. If everything goes well, then no problem, but when things go wrong, hedge funds can be a very frustrating investment.

That said, there are a few things you should know that will help you steer clear of danger.

Hedge funds are misnamed. Most of them don't "hedge" at all. They instead tend to be focused bets on very narrow slices of a sector or industry. They can also be exceptionally broad, giving the investment manager the ability to buy anything on the planet.

If you're considering a hedge fund, check to see if the investment objective and investment parameters have any limitations on them at all. If not, your money could end up being used for a Peruvian brothel or a wind farm in Africa.

Also, hedge funds are typically set up as partnerships (as I mentioned earlier), where investors become limited partners. They're not corporations where investors become shareholders. Because these are partnership interests, there's no marketplace where you can go to sell your investment. Usually you have to sell the interests back to the partnership itself, which might or might not want to buy it. So cashing out can be a challenge.

While the partnership might not want to buy your interests back, typically the operating agreement lists out the conditions under which the hedge fund has to cash you out. Pay particular attention to these details… they are important!

And understand the terms…

First, there is a "Lock Up." That is the initial period during which you can't get your money back. This can be anywhere from a day (very unusual) to 18 months. The normal lock up is a year.

Think about that.

You'll be separated from your money for at least a year. After that, you have to request redemption at the end of a calendar quarter, and usually you must make the request at least 45 days, if not 90 days, in advance.

There is no selling on the day you feel bad about the markets, or just want your money back for other purposes. You have to plan on when you want the funds returned.

Then there's the "Gate."

Normally people don't want out of good performing funds, they want out of bad ones. The problem is that if too many investors want out at the same time, then the manager has to sell assets rapidly, which could force down the value of whatever it is he holds. This is particularly true if the investment manager has invested in illiquid assets like real estate or art, or thinly traded securities.

If too many people ask for redemption at the same time, usually more than 10% of the fund, the manager can throw down a "gate," and only redeem a small percentage of all requests, holding off on the rest of the requests until a later date. This is fully at the discretion of the manager.

The last term of note is "in-kind." That's almost a bad four-letter word in the investment community. If a hedge fund is holding a bunch of illiquid, poorly performing assets, and many investors want out, the hedge fund manager can send investors their share of the investments instead of cash.

So if a hedge fund manager is holding notes on a bunch of real estate that no one wants and he gets overrun with redemption requests, he can send you your share of the notes. As an investor, you now have to deal with trying to get a bid and get out of this stuff.

All of these things come into play in hedge funds, but (with the exception of K-1s on Master Limited Partnerships) don't apply to what we think of as traditional stock and bond investments.

There is a reason hedge fund investments are limited to accredited investors. People should be financially and legally sophisticated before locking up their money in such vehicles.

Think about all the documents put in front of you for signature in everyday life: credit card applications, mortgages, membership applications, school documents for kids, car loans, etc. Do you really read them all? Do you know what you're liable for and the consequences if something goes wrong?

If you don't typically read fine print, and you're not comfortable giving some manager the ability to do whatever he or she wants with your money, then steer clear! It could be one of the best "decide-not-to-invest" decisions you'll ever make.

Do You Keep Your Cash Here?

July, 2013

"You want me to wake up at four in the morning to call you in sick tomorrow?"

"Well, yeah. I've got to skip school so I can judge at the Crisco pie-making contest in Orlando. It's FREE pie, dad!"

I was having this conversation with my 18-year-old son. I was in Mexico, speaking at the Sovereign Society's Total Wealth Symposium and he needed my help.

So, what did I do?

Before I answer, let me build my defense here…

The Rational Man Theory that mainstream economists advocate says that people, when faced with a choice, will do what's right for themselves. In other words, each consumer will make a rational decision when faced with a tradeoff about their situation.

Really? I beg to differ.

Take money market accounts for example. They're a great idea, right? I imagine most everybody reading this has money in a money market account.

And you're getting slaughtered, aren't you?

Your money market accounts earn nothing. In fact, it earns a good 1.5% less than inflation.

Now, the Rational Man Theory says you should take all your money out of your money market accounts and go buy stuff. But you're not doing that, are you? Why not? Because, the reality is, we're really an irrational species.

We do stupid things all the time, like keeping our cash in our underperforming money market accounts… or rushing into the markets at the peak of a boom… or waking up at 4 a.m. in a Mexican hotel to call a Tampa school principal (yes, I did it)…

There's definitely a better way to understand the economy and what happens than using the Rational Man Theory. Quite simply: Understand what drives people.

What motivates you to take out your credit card or cash and actually do something with it?

What motivates you to buy a bigger house, take out a bigger mortgage and leverage yourself to your eyeballs?

What motivates you to make irrational decisions?

Thanks to our 20 years of research into demographic trends and consumer spending, we have the answer to those questions. It's our children.

Children make us do stupid things.

They push us to make irrational decisions. Admittedly, those decisions are occasionally rational, but mostly not. These irrational decisions influence how we spend our money.

And because, generationally speaking, we follow predictable spending patterns as we age, this knowledge becomes useful. For example, when a generation reaches the age and stage of life where they have children, you'll notice a boom in baby furniture. When those kids go off to school, you'll see a boom in stationary supplies. When they're about 14 years old, you'll see a boom in the potato chip industry. That's us, as parents, buying tons of chips for our ravenous kids.

This tells us something about the years ahead...

The biggest generation in America — the baby boomers — is now solidly in the empty-nester stage of life. They're past the time in life where their children are driving them to make irrational decisions. At this point, their children are still out hunting for a partner with which to repeat the whole cycle for themselves.

Now the parents are on to the next financial stage, which is saving every last nickel for retirement, hence the reason no one is busy pulling money out of money market accounts, no matter how little they pay!

The lesson for all of us watching these trends unfold is not to expect a boom in consumer spending just around the corner, no matter how hard the Fed tries to pull on this rope, or how much the press gabs about the recovery.

Be suspect of the markets because, as the last several months have shown, they're based on the smoke and mirrors of the Fed printing, not a lasting, dynamic, consumption-driven recovery. For that to happen, we'd have to see millions of people making what the Fed and the government tell us are rational economic decisions... which isn't going to happen.

We're smarter than that.

A Tough Time to be Average

August, 2013

In 2003, when my son was in elementary school, I received a note from his science teacher. It turned out he had chosen not to turn in a project and write a paper. These were deliberate choices, as his teacher had reminded him they were due.

I was unhappy, to say the least.

When I pointed out that he currently had a C in the class and that I was angry, he was confused. "A 72 is still passing, right?" he asked. "Of course it's still passing, but you can do better!" I (kind of) yelled at him. "If a C is not a good grade, then why is it passing?" he asked.

Dang it. I was put on the defensive by the logic of a 10-year-old. I hate it when that happens.

From there I had to go through all of the reasons why earning an average grade would count for almost nothing.

Yes, it would allow him to pass from one grade to the next, but it would not give him the freedom of choices that come with exceptional grades, and it would earn him none of the satisfaction and accolades that accompany high achievement.

He remained unimpressed, but he responded quite well when I outlined the punishments for what I consider to be poor grades.

All of this came to mind as I read the financial papers at the end of the second quarter of 2013. There were loads of articles touting the returns of the major indices, with much gloating about how buy-and-hold investors, particularly those that simply buy index funds and hang on, have done so well during the year.

Hmmm.

It struck me that this point of view is really in favor when the markets are up, particularly when there's been a multi-year positive run... but what happens next?

We're in year five of a market clearly distorted by the actions of the Federal Reserve. While there are certainly arguments about the size of the distortion, there should be zero debate about the fact the distortion exists.

This artificial boost to the equity markets has resulted in all-time highs for indices across the board.

Both of these things — Fed intervention, which could be on the verge of slowing, and markets at such high levels — should be seen as huge, flashing warning signs. Yet market pundits tout that readers and listeners should abandon all analysis and simply jump on the buy-and-hold index train.

From where we stand, it looks like that train will derail. And even if it doesn't, is it worth the potential risk to your wealth?

We would love for buy-and-hold investing to work because it would be so simple. Investors would have no need of financial analysis, and major chunks of Wall Street — from analysts to salesmen to traders — could be dismantled. What's the point of providing research or persuasion if buying a boring basket provides a decent outcome?

The problem comes down to timing. While buy-and-hold, on average, might work out in the long run, there can be substantial periods where such an approach would lead to disaster.

There was an entire decade (the 1970s) where buy-and-hold was death for a portfolio. Shorter periods, like the early 1980s, the early 2000s and, of course, the recent financial crisis were equally damaging.

The unspoken caveat of buy-and-hold, or average investing, is that it works out as long as you don't need the money. If, during a down period, you can leave the funds invested, then it might work out. Maybe.

But how many investors are in such a position? How many people can take the attitude that if their portfolio tanks, they can simply leave it for as long as it takes — a year, two years, or a decade — until it recovers?

I guess such investors can exist, but if they do, they must be few and far between. Most of the investors I meet are more cautious with their funds, and would rather not see their portfolios fall in value for an extended period of time.

With corporate earnings tepid, GDP growth weak, the markets near all-time highs and the Fed's plans in question, now looks like a pretty good time not to be average.

A Nobel Prize for Saying Ignorance is Bliss?

October, 2013

On Monday, October 14, 2013, the Royal Swedish Academy of Sciences awarded Professors Fama and Hansen of the University of Chicago, and Professor Shiller of Yale University, the Nobel Prize for Economic Sciences.

Let's start with the first two recipients of the award...

Mr. Fama's contribution to the world was to tell us that we can't beat the markets because they immediately incorporate all known information. In other words, the Efficient Markets theory.

Mr. Hansen developed methods of testing asset prices.

Now I'm certain that this news was well received in many corners of the investment world, including the Vanguard headquarters, a company that built an empire out of index investing.

After all, Mr. Fama's Efficient Markets theory allows people to wash their hands of any responsibility for their investment decisions since they can't beat the markets anyway. Instead, just buy an index fund and then hope and pray it goes in the right direction.

Hmmm.

What happens if the index funds are falling when you need the money?

Oh, that's right. I remember now: You just adjust your time frame.

I'm sure the news was met with a different sort of reaction from other corners of the investment world...

Like in the basement of the New York Stock Exchange, where high-frequency trading companies place their computers within spitting distance of the exchange's computers.

This physical arrangement allows the trading firms to see information milliseconds ahead of everyone else, place trades accordingly, and earn profits from it.

Yes, that sounds very, very efficient.

I imagine these guys were giggling in their Fruit Loops about the Nobel Prize this year.

Then there's the third winner: Yale's Professor Shiller.

He made a name for himself by warning of the housing collapse... and the tech stocks collapse. He pointed out asset bubbles and the mania that can extend from the psychology of investing when prices continue to grow.

So, two of this year's Nobel Prize winners say resistance is futile (a Star Trek reference), and the third one claims that bubbles happen.

While these gentlemen create a lot of good analysis, I'm still searching for the piece that moves us farther along.

To say that people won't do any better by making active decisions in the markets, and that bubbles occur, seems to be at odds. If everything is known immediately, then how can bubbles happen? If bubbles occur, then aren't we better served by stepping aside ahead of time, or at least having a strategy for exiting when things go south?

How about a Nobel Prize for recognizing that government entities that work hard to ensure profits for the banks by keeping the yield curve steep, greatly influence the markets while harming the rest of us?

How about a Nobel Prize for pointing out that owning an index fund is great as long as you want to be guaranteed average returns and 100% of the risk?

What about the notion that buying non-correlated equities (things that don't usually move together) is a wonderful idea on a normal day, but when fear sets in all equities move in the same direction... down!

I'd support a Nobel Prize for that piece of work.

Obviously I'm not a fan of the Efficient Markets theory. I've seen — and written about — too many instances where the efficiencies are either non-existent or are systematically removed from the marketplace.

What else do you call it when the Fed holds a secret meeting and demands all participants take bailout money SPECIFICALLY so that investors can't determine who is bust and who is not?

The "efficient market" was on display when Bank of America and Citi were teetering on the edge of failure. Then they were whisked into the arms of the government with tens of billions in bailout money.

And which sector of equities, exactly, held up during the crisis?

What happened to all of those wonderful models that showed crisscrossing lines, cancelling out each other's risk while earning average returns?

Oh, that's right...

They all took a nosedive.

So did every piece of fixed income, except U.S. Treasurys.

I know I'm mixing Efficient Markets, Irrational Exuberance, and Modern Portfolio Theory into the same pot.

But I think investors have been sold a framework that doesn't work very well for them. Instead, it provides an awful lot of benefit to the purveyors of the "sell" side.

"Buy what we have," they say.

"There are no advantages," they tell us... except for the ones they provide to each other or sell to the highest bidder.

How to Tell the Difference Between a Dying and Thriving Company

January, 2014

One of the perks of living close to the office is that I get to go home for lunch. Most days my wife and I chit chat, discussing current news and our schedule. But every once in a while I'm at home alone for lunch and I turn on the TV. I'm immediately depressed, and it's not because of the programming. It's the commercials.

I've not studied the demographics of those who watch TV at noon on a weekday, but judging from the commercials it must be a combination of people who have been in an auto accident, been fired, never attended college or even finished high school and are currently unemployed or under-employed, or are really old.

And they all share one common trait… they're gullible. The ads are outrageous!

When it comes to commercials touting for-profit colleges, they always scream: "Invest in yourself!"

I think I will, by *not* sending them money.

But that line got me thinking about how companies spend money…

It used to be that mature companies would pay dividends, using their cash-cow products to generate returns that benefited stockholders.

Young companies with great growth potential would plow any revenue back into research and development or fund growth in some other way.

Companies that were in the middle — established but still growing — would typically use their cash to grow through acquisition, upgrade their systems and equipment, and perhaps pay a small dividend as well.

All of this made sense. However, there is now a new use of corporate cash that's getting a lot of attention. That is, buying one's own stock.

Corporate buybacks aren't new, but they were once relegated to companies that were more or less dying, or at least in a dying industry. After exhausting all other possibilities, company management would concede that it simply had no good alternatives and would buy its own stock.

Today, corporate buybacks are viewed a bit differently. Instead of signaling the death of a company or industry, they tell investors that companies are in it for themselves, or at least their shareholders and management.

It's no secret that consumers haven't bounced back with a vengeance, or that the economy is growing at a tepid pace, at best. Still, corporate America has been able to contain costs (read here: hold wages down) and thereby keep earnings on track, even if they aren't growing dramatically.

Meanwhile, interest rates are exceptionally low. So companies are earning cash and can borrow cheaply, but they're cautious about expanding because overall economic growth is sluggish at best.

So what does one do to keep the wheels of finance — and earnings per share (EPS) — turning? Why, use cash and borrowed money to reduce the number of shares outstanding, of course!

If earnings remain the same, but the number of shares is reduced, then EPS must go higher. Technically, each share isn't worth any more, since the company used cash on hand or borrowed money to fund the purchase. However, because EPS goes up, a key measure of the health of the company suddenly improves. This makes the shares of the company more attractive to investors, which tends to drive up the share price.

In addition to making the shares more attractive, a rising EPS also rewards management. Of the 30 stocks in the Dow Jones Industrials Average, 26 use EPS as one of the measurements when setting executive compensation.

So how popular are corporate buybacks?

In 2013, the 30 companies in the Dow authorized over $200 billion in stock buybacks, or almost three times what they spent on research and development. It appears that the trend of buying one's own stock has caught on.

I'm not saying it's wrong or bad for a company to buy back its own stock. Apple is a great example of when this makes sense.

The company is huge. It has a market capitalization of almost half a trillion dollars. It generates tens of billions of dollars in free cash flow. With all of that green coming in, Apple has to make choices. Does it try to invest that money, or pay dividends (which it has), or buy back stock? In this case, the answer is all three.

That being said, there are times when a stock buyback is a sign of trouble.

Companies with falling revenue, shrinking earnings, and little prospect for growth will sometimes buy back their own stock to keep the price up.

The trick you need to learn is to be able to spot the difference.

Some companies track this exact thing. Trim Tabs, out of Sausalito, California, has made a business of tracking corporate financials. One of its measurements is called "Float Shrink," which watches the change in the number of shares of a company held outside of the company.

Trim Tabs has even created an exchange-traded fund to buy shares of companies that are healthy and growing, yet buying back their own shares… like Apple.

In a crazy world where economies seem sickly at best, yet companies are booking strong profits, it helps to have a variety of ways of figuring out which companies have the best chance of a rising stock price.

If they appear healthy and are screaming "I invest in myself!" then they could be a good choice.

U.S. DOLLAR

Airplanes and the Purchasing Power of the U.S. Dollar

November, 2012

I started my working life on Wall Street, first in a management training program and then on a bond desk. When you get to a trading desk, the first thing you have to learn is the rhythm of whatever security you trade. In bonds, the rhythm wasn't too hard.

Lesson #1: Don't fight the Fed. They have more money than anyone else.

Lesson #2: Stand up and hold your arms out like an airplane. Pretend one "wing" is the price of the bond and the other "wing" is the yield. When one dips, the other rises and vice versa.

That's it.

Now imagine a group of 20-something-year-old hot shots who think they're cool new traders standing around in designer suits pretending they're airplanes. You get the picture.

This lesson in prices/yields recently came to mind when I was asked for the eight-millionth time about the U.S. dollar. You know the story…

Given that the Federal Reserve has launched not one, not two, but THREE rounds of quantitative easing, where they create money from nothing — and by the way, the third round has no defined end — doesn't the dollar have to go down!?

Clearly, when there are more dollars created then all the rest lose value, so the Fed's efforts must, and I say MUST, lead to devaluation… right?

Wrong.

You've got the wrong airplane in mind.

To figure out what will happen to the U.S. dollar, you can use the same exercise that I was forced to use when determining the movement of prices versus yields on bonds. Stand up or, for those a bit more sedentary, simply stay in your chair, and put your arms out like an airplane.

One "wing" is the value or purchasing power of the U.S. dollar, and the other "wing" is NOT... I repeat, NOT... the number of dollars we print or are in circulation. Instead, the other "wing" is the value of foreign currencies.

Given that there are numerous foreign currencies, sitting might be better so you can put out a foot to represent another currency.

If you think about it, we don't price dollars against other dollars. When we talk about more dollars being created leading to lower purchasing power, the unspoken qualifying statement is, "with all things being held constant." Of course, this alludes to the purchasing power of all other currencies being held steady.

This is the myth of currencies and central banks. They're always in flux. The value of a currency is not a simple outcome of activities inside the country. It's a combination of all activities inside the country compared to the combination of all activities inside another country.

The actual exchange rate is simply the numerical representation of how people view the complex items on any given day. Our situation today is a great example.

Inside the U.S. we sort of suck. Coming off the worst economic downturn in a generation, we have wheezing economic growth at 2% or less, wages are low, prices are rising, and the fed continues printing new money (figuratively) while manipulating interest rates lower.

By any rational measure, the U.S. dollar should be in free fall.

HOWEVER...

Using the airplane analogy from above, if the U.S. dollar is in one hand and the euro in the other, which one should go up and which one should go down?

The euro must be on the downside. With Greece in bankruptcy and Spain not far behind, the very existence of the euro is in question. To hold it for a storehouse of value would be a fool's game.

Now do the same with the yen. With a debt-to-GDP of 230%, a rapidly aging population that is literally dying off, and a young set that doesn't want to work or marry, who wants to hold the yen?

Once we change the measure of the U.S. dollar from "how many are out there?" to "what would you rather have instead?" it's easy to see how the U.S. dollar could, and should, remain quite strong in the months and even years ahead.

This doesn't mean the U.S. dollar is golden.

We're still a very weak economy. If the euro zone countries or Japan radically improve their economies, we could see a huge swing in the value of the dollar. But I'm not willing to bet my savings on it.

We're still the best looking beast in an ugly dog contest.

Why Should You Stash Your Strong U.S. Dollars at EverBank?

June, 2012

In May 2011, I presented at the World Currency Watch Conference in La Jolla, CA. The theme of the conference was "how to deal with the demise of the U.S. dollar." I had a different point of view. I felt the dollar would get stronger... an opinion that was in the minority. In fact, out of 500 attendees and roughly 20 presenters, I was the *only* one who believed this.

So why was I being so contrary?

I wasn't banking on the U.S. becoming a shining light of fiscal conservation. I didn't see the currency-manipulator-in-chief at the time, Ben Bernanke suddenly ending his damaging ways.

What I saw on the horizon was a world filled with bad currency, where the U.S. was simply the mildest offender. When the other two large currencies available are the yen and the euro, the U.S. dollar looks pretty good by comparison.

Face it, in the world of currency, it's a beauty contest, not a measure of value. And sometimes we don't vote for the prettiest. We vote against the ugliest.

That is where the U.S. dollar stands today. It's a tattered wisp of what it used to be in terms of absolute value, but a real looker when compared to the other choices.

While the past year has affirmed my view of how the dollar will fare in world markets — it was up about 6% at the time of writing — I didn't address how investors should store the dollars I suggested they accumulate. We've been telling *Boom & Bust* readers to develop streams of income wherever possible as well.

This has proved easier said than done, particularly for short-term liquidity. With a one-year U.S. Treasury yielding just above zero, the ability to earn any yield on short-term funds, and still keep them relatively safe, has been near impossible.

Well, not anymore.

Erika Nolan, publisher of the Sovereign Society sent me a note about the offering she had wrung out of EverBank. Given the long relationship between the two organizations, and probably a little bit due to her persistence and enthusiasm for them to create such a product, EverBank made available a Yield Pledge Money Market Account with a bonus rate of 1.35%, resulting in a 1.06% APY (average percentage yield) in the first year.

This is the highest I've seen, and is offered from a company with which we've had the pleasure of working in the past. And because of our own relationship with both EverBank and the Sovereign Society, we are able to make this product available to you as well.

We currently live in a world where terms like financial repression and negative yield are the norm, and it appears things will get worse before they get better. It's nice to know that you have an option for storing your hard earned dollars where they'll provide some growth while Rome burns, Athens crumbles, and Tokyo tanks.

MARKETS

Financial Markets Could End Up in the "Irons"

September, 2012

Living in Florida is different. We think cold weather is anything under 60 degrees. We see flip-flops as perfectly acceptable business casual dress. And many of us get to sail every week.

Each of these things shapes our reality, but sailing does something different. It adds vernacular to daily conversation. As I look at the financial markets and reflect on the forces at work, I keep coming back to the same term — the "irons."

Sail boats don't go upwind, so what happens if that is where you need to go?

A sailboat has to go "close to the wind," which means the skipper will point the boat 20 degrees off where the wind is coming from. This allows the boat to move forward, but it also means the boat is moving slightly away from the intended destination.

Because of this, every so often the skipper will have to "tack," which is to change direction when moving upwind. If done correctly, this maneuver is seamless and has a wonderful flow. If done poorly, a boat can end up in "irons…"

What is the dreaded "irons?" That's when the boat is pointed directly upwind, not in the skipper's control, and it's being pushed straight backward.

This is *not* good.

It's also exactly what seems to be happening in personal finance today.

The wind is the combined global economy. Currently 80% of the world is in a manufacturing recession at the very least (the U.S. included)… and in an all-out recession at worst.

This doesn't serve the purpose of investors whose goals include growing and protecting their portfolios.

The Federal Reserve is the wily puff of wind that comes up suddenly from the back of the boat. It gives a little bit of lift but not enough to get the boat cruising in the proper direction. That feat takes strategy.

Investors are the skipper of their financial boat. Most of them simply try to tough out the prevailing winds, hoping that if they wait long enough the wind will change direction.

But what if it doesn't?

What if this weather pattern stays for a while?

For all of you who've found yourself in irons on a boat, one of the best ways to resolve this is to use the backward momentum of the boat in your favor. Hold the tiller over to starboard or port about 60 degrees, and then be patient. The boat will come around soon enough, then you can adjust your sails and be on your way!

For those working on their personal finances, there's another choice. Instead of simply hoping for the wind to change, you can take a new approach to the situation and leave the world of hopeful growth to others.

The new tack is to steer towards the income-producing equities, those with very nice dividends in sectors or industries with plenty of business... even when the storms arrive. If you position yourself in this arena, not only will you get further ahead, but you'll make better time to your destination AND have the peace of mind to sleep at night.

Hate the General Equity Markets?

August, 2012

How come all the financial-advice commercials show smiling, happy people on the beach… or looking smug at their personal computers? Where are the real people?

Where are the people that bust their butts all day at work, worry about their kids, or parents, or both, and then, with their last lucid thought of the day, worry about their wealth?

Where are the people who are angry at bailed-out billionaires, trillion-dollar debts and the printing of new money? They know that, in some way, all of these things will take cash out of their pockets.

I think we need a reality show for angry savers.

Then we need a revolt.

Given the manipulation of the forces that drive equity prices — things like interest rates and propped-up companies — we should be angry. Spitting mad, in fact.

We're being forced to play a game where the rules are no longer fair and we can't trust the game master anymore. It's like finding out your uncles are cheating in your game of poker and they won't let you leave the table until you're bankrupt. It seems they've super-glued you to your chair, so what choice do you have?

Well, I'm here to tell you: There's always a choice…

While equity markets have been on a tear lately, there's a wall of worry that is tall and steep (and rightly so). The euro zone is in a recession, with the U.S. not far behind. China is slowing down.

On home soil, our fiscal cliff is edging closer, unemployment is high, and we're one Fed announcement away from… what? Saving grace? The last straw?

This isn't a world in which we should simply buy equities, diversify, and hope. That's a recipe for wealth destruction.

There's a better way, but it involves work, which is why most people won't do it. But that's OK. It leaves a little more for the rest of us.

This is a Call to Action

This is a call to action for those who are fed up with the rollercoaster of hope and fear in the general equity markets. Instead of staying on the ride because you feel you have no choice, get off now and focus on the income side of the ledger. Not necessarily bonds, although there are some that make sense.

Instead, look further afield. Focus on stocks that pay handsome dividends that operate in growing markets. Areas like health care and multi-family real estate trusts are great hunting grounds. That's where we've made some solid returns in our Boom & Bust portfolio.

There are other areas worth considering as well, like energy trusts and energy transport companies. The income streams from these types of investments are in the 6% to 10% range, well beyond what you could get on a bond. They also have the distinct advantage of getting investors away from the "did it go up or down today?" game.

So go ahead, roll up your sleeves and dive into the research. The goal is to find companies that are in growth industries supported by the aging boomers, are growing and profitable, and pay a respectable stream of income. That's our main goal each month in *Boom & Bust*.

From there, you're just a few investments away from thumbing your nose at just about everyone on CNBC and at the Fed. That's a pretty good feeling.

BANKS

Banks are Hoarding Their Excess Reserves From the Fed

October, 2012

I give a lot of speeches, as well as radio and TV interviews. One of the hardest parts about that is making sure that my comments are suited to the audience — not too wonky, but not simplistic either.

When the topic of the Federal Reserve and new money comes up, I always have to couch my comments in a certain way. I can't simply say, "when the Fed prints money," because someone, somewhere, will start jumping up and down like Arnold Horshack on "Welcome Back, Kotter," desperate to call me out.

The Fed doesn't really print money. Fine. Instead it boosts electronic balances.

That leads to a problem. Unless those ones and zeroes are converted into cash, the recovery goes nowhere, and the Fed fails.

Welcome to the game. Here's how it's played...

The Fed doesn't print money in any sense. The U.S. Treasury controls the U.S. Mint. The Fed controls the flow of funds, but it must do so through banks. That's because the Fed is neither federal — it is not an agency of the national government — nor is it a reserve — it holds no balance of funds.

The Fed's only way to reach the market is through its owners, which happen to be the private banks.

National U.S. banks, such as Bank of America, Citibank, Wells Fargo, etc., are required to be part of the Federal Reserve system. As such, they have an account at the Fed where they hold their excess reserves. It's through these accounts that the Fed changes the amount of "money" in the financial system.

If the Fed wants to take money out of the system, it sells bonds to one of its member banks. Through this transaction the member bank receives the bonds and hands over cash to the Fed, removing money from the pool that's sloshing around the economy.

The reverse is also true. To inject money into the system, the Fed buys a security from a member bank, which takes the security (a bond, for example) out of circulation and puts more money into circulation... almost.

The Fed accomplishes the increase in money by simply adjusting the bank's reserve account higher. It's a keystroke. Nothing physical changes hands.

But after that, the Fed has no control. If the bank doesn't put the new funds to use in some way, then nothing happens.

Yes, a security was removed from the financial sector, but the corresponding pop in useable funds is now simply an entry in the bank's reserve account. Who really cares?

Before the financial crisis, the total balance of excess reserves — the amount above what banks are required to hold at the Fed — was around $60 billion. Now excess reserves are over $2 trillion.

It's one of those things that make you go, "Hmmm."

Inflationists point out that when these extra dollars are changed from dormant digits into real cash through lending, prices will explode.

Well, that could happen. But what if it doesn't? What if banks, those paragons of quality lending standards, hold onto the funds because (1) there aren't enough strong lending opportunities to warrant risking capital, and (2) they are scared witless about their existing books of loans that still include millions of foreclosed homes and millions of worthless home equity lines of credit (HELOCs)?

(Of course, this is what they're doing... Bank of America is a great example as it just got sued for $1 billion because of its sloppy lending.)

Well, you get an explosion in excess reserves.

This started three and a half years ago*. You would think that 40 months would be long enough to see some sort of boom in lending and prices... if it were going to happen.

Our view remains the same — banks are hoarding the cash... er, electronic entries... to guard against their own troubles. We have *not* deleveraged. We have not dealt with our solvency crisis.

Like some Japanese B-movie, so far the banks have simply eaten the Fed's pet monster while no-one else had gotten a taste.

* Now five and a half years ago.

BONDS

How Safe are Government Bonds Really?

June, 2012

Now *that's* an interesting question.

Typically a saver doesn't "pay" to keep his money safe. A saver simply deposits money into the bank and then collects paltry interest.

But what would you do when simply stashing money in the bank is not an option? What if the worry is not theft in the physical form, but overall devaluation of the money itself? You would have to choose another way to hold your wealth.

And that is where the problem lies.

If you have a few million dollars or euros to safeguard, chances are you would diligently pursue a strategy of diversification. You'd put some funds in different banks and denominate your holdings into different currencies. But what if you had hundreds of millions, or even billions of dollars? What could you do to protect yourself?

A simple savings account won't do, so you might look to bonds. You could buy debt, or more specifically, government debt. But from what government?

Which particular government bonds do you think has the least credit risk? Will it pursue a strategy aimed at devaluing your funds? Does it also have a large enough capital market to accept your incoming billions without disruption, and have financial laws that allow cross-border transactions?

At the end of the day, it's easy to spot the favorite choices because their interest rates have fallen dramatically…

The U.S., for all of its troubles, remains a top choice for those wanting to stash their excess cash. With an inflation rate of 2.3%, and the current yield on a two-year U.S. Treasury bond hovering around 0.25%, buyers of these government bonds are accepting a 2.05% loss of purchasing.

This is essentially the same as paying the U.S. government to hold your money for several years, simply being happy you can actually retrieve it at the appointed time. Of course, if inflation falls, then your negative rate of return could shrink.

Now the German government has joined the party. It has finally recognized the incredible investor demand for safety-regardless-of-interest and has issued a 2-year bond that pays zero… nada… zip. A buyer of this bond will receive no interest whatsoever. And he'll see the investment fall in purchasing power by the rate of inflation, which is currently 1.9%.

And then there's Switzerland…

This country is quite the conundrum. Investors believed the Swiss franc was so close to being backed by gold that they dumped euros and bought Swiss francs by the bucket in 2011. This caused the cost of Swiss goods (watches, machinery, etc.) to skyrocket, threatening exports and tourism. As a measure of how expensive the currency had become, if you exchanged dollars and bought Swiss francs to buy a Big Mac, it would have cost you $17.50!

But back to our interest rate conversation.

The Swiss have long recognized that investors buy government bonds for different reasons. As such, the Swiss do not limit their interest rates to merely positive rates, or even zero. The Swiss allow their bonds to be bought at less than zero interest.

Recently the country sold bills at -0.62%, so for every one million Swiss francs you invested, you'd only get back 993,800. Brilliant! This takes the idea of "negative rates of return" to new heights!

Of course, in keeping with the math of the other two examples, we must consider Switzerland's rate of inflation. Over the past year, prices in Switzerland have actually fallen by 0.99%. It has experienced deflation.

Think about how weird this is. In the country seen as the ultimate in safety, they issue bonds that charge the investor interest (-0.62%). At the same time, there is deflation (-0.99%). The result is a positive rate of return in Switzerland of 0.37%. We live in strange times indeed.

So what are you to do with your money? Where should you put your money to keep it safe?

That depends on many different factors… but your first step should be to know what options you have.

4.375% Interest... Tax Free. THIS is What Investors Should be Looking For

September, 2013

It's no secret that the city of Detroit is bankrupt. While union officials and other creditors might disagree, there's no way to look at the city's assets and liabilities and reach any other conclusion.

In the world of common sense, it would be foolish to lend the city money. This explains why Detroit isn't trying to access the municipal bond markets at the moment. Instead, it's simply not paying its creditors and hoarding all its cash.

But are those entities that are close to — but still not a part of — Detroit behaving in the same way?

Well...

No.

Recently, the Detroit Public School System (DPSS) went looking for cash.

It's common for schools to issue short-term notes as they wait on payment from some other entity, like the state or federal government. Typically, these are one-year notes and are specifically secured by the reimbursement in question.

DPSS issued $92 million worth of one-year notes specifically backed by its expected payment from the state of Michigan.

To ensure that potential bondholders were comfortable with this offer, the school district wrote into the offering that the payment from the state would not go directly to the school district. Instead, the funds would first go to bondholders, with any remaining funds allocated to the district.

Also, the district is required to set aside funds each month to ensure that it makes its debt payments. All of this led Standard & Poor's to give the bond deal a rating of SP-1, the second highest short-term rating.

So, with all of that backing, what is the interest rate on this debt?

4.375%.

Tax-free.

At the 39.5% tax bracket, that makes this the equivalent of receiving 7.11% on a taxable security. Remember, this is a one-year note. And this is at a time when 20-year junk bonds are yielding just over 6%.

DPSS's problem is clear. It shares a name with a certain city that has a financial issue. That's not to say the Detroit Public School System is a bastion of financial responsibility. In fact, the district is in such woefully bad shape the state took it over. But that's not the point.

The point is that the investors who saw this bond offering for what it was — a one-year note backed by payments from Michigan that have already been signed over — are going to win.

In a day and age when the Federal Reserve has done all it can to take interest out of the pockets of savers — and the federal government has done all it can to tax the rest — receiving 4.375% interest for a year is a heck of a deal.

***This* is the sort of thing investors should be trying to find.**

There is no doubt that, in bond-trading terminology, this issue has hair on it because of the district's name and history. Yet with the solid backing of the state, repayment is all but assured.

As time goes on there should be more deals like this in muni-bond land, where issuers have names similar to issuers that have gone under, or are on the brink of financial ruin. This is where homework pays off handsomely!

Of course, there are losers in this equation, specifically the families and workers in the Detroit Public School System.

There is no doubt that the 4.375% interest rate on this one-year note is exceptionally high and out of line with the risk involved. What should it be?

In May of 2012 DPSS issued a one-year note at 1.25%. Obviously rates have moved up since then. If we assume a 0.5% rate increase, which is wildly too much for the move in one-year interest rates, DPSS's cost of financing would move up to 1.75%.

The additional interest the district has to pay (4.375% – 1.75%, or 2.625% of $92 million), adds up to $2.415 million. This is money that will not be available to the district to educate kids or pay for services. This is clearly the downside of having a poor history of financial management and sharing geography and a name with what is the largest municipal bankruptcy in U.S. history.

So as we go through the next several years of financial turmoil in city and state financing, be on the lookout for extraordinary deals like the one above.

Another issuer that just hit our radar is the island of Puerto Rico. With a crushing debt load and little appetite for stronger financial oversight, the municipal markets are punishing the island state.

There could exist in the trash heap a bond issue or two that have solid revenue streams apart from the general budget but are getting thrown away because they share a name with the state.

And all it takes to find such gems is some old-fashioned research.

Why the Stock Market is Like Vegas

October, 2012

Occasionally I have to go to Vegas on business. I hate it.

The place teems with people trying to be excited about the possibility of winning big but all the while losing. They must be losing, or else Vegas wouldn't exist.

As I point out to my kids on a regular basis, Las Vegas is a monument to stupid people who return often to pay their respects.

There must be some sort of homing signal buried in the desert that beckons people who are bad at math. I know there are some winners. Some people who have figured out a way to consistently (if not every time) go home with a little more money than they started with, but that is a very small minority.

Over the last several years, the stock market has taken on the same qualities as Vegas…

It used to be that investors would spend hours toiling over whatever branch of investment-selection analysis they favored, typically technical or fundamental. Or they would obsessively gather data on the particular market they favored, like bonds or precious metals.

All of this made sense, right up until 2009.

Since then the game in town has been one of estimating government action and central bank action… then estimating the reaction to that action.

It has all the trappings of one of those endless conversations that seem to start with: "Well, I know that you know that I know that you know…"

So What's An Investor To Do?

The first thing to do is recognize where we are.

The economies of the world don't support the current levels of the stock market. Most major economies are in or near recession, yet the U.S. equity markets are at multi-year highs.

Inflation is running just under 2% and yet 10-year Treasurys are at 1.73%. Money is too cheap.

China is slowing.

Japan is slowing.

Europe is, well, Europe.

But here's the problem: Unlike Vegas, once you realize the craziness of the situation, you can't very well get on a plane and "leave" investing. Most of us still want or need to grow our assets… so we must constantly work to avoid the pitfalls and take advantage of the opportunities.

Pitfall: The Growth Story

Growth at a time like this?

Really?!?

Don't fall for the "growth" story.

I get so many calls from young investors who ask if they should be in growth stocks — those in typically high flying sectors like tech. I don't blame them for asking this question. They're young.

I always answer with a question of my own: Which amendment to the U.S. Constitution stipulates young investors must buy risky stuff?

This hocus pocus was thought up by the investment community to absolve themselves of any responsibility for choosing what to own.

Using a very — VERY — long-time horizon, it can be shown that equities in growth industries have more risk and provide greater return than others. Of course, if your own investment horizon is less than 25 or 30 years, this might not be your own experience.

Besides, doesn't it make more sense to buy investments that seem to offer a positive return and an appropriate amount of risk for that return given the current economy? The point is to understand that a one-page questionnaire addressing your age and risk tolerance has nothing to do with how investments will work out over the next year, or two, or even five.

Choose better.

Opportunity: Hedge

.alked about this before and we will again... and again...

ιrrent economic and investment environment is distorted. Capital markets are looking to government intervention for price support. Trading platforms are the domain of high frequency trading firms that place and cancel thousands of orders a day. The system is rife with danger.

So hedge.

We use long investments and short investments in the *Boom & Bust* portfolio.

Many people use options, as Adam O'Dell does with *Cycle 9 Alert*.

Whatever your strategy, use a methodical approach to guard against catastrophic loss.

Sadly, we're one flash crash or one "bad" government announcement away from a 15% or 20% drop that could quickly turn into a rout.

INCOME

Fixed Income May Not be a Viable Path Anymore

October, 2012

There's an old story about how much Michael Jordan made as a basketball player… it was something like $80,000 per minute of play.

His rewards for "simply" playing a game were made to seem like the stuff of legend. The story ended by pointing out that if Michael Jordan wanted to have as much money as Bill Gates, he'd have to work for over 200 years.

The moral of the story? Geeks win.

But while this might be true for personal fortunes, it can't be said for power.

Goldman Sachs and JP Morgan control hundreds of billions of dollars. Apple is worth over $600 billion and brings in cash by the wheelbarrow full. But none of them are the mightiest wielder of power. Instead, that honor goes to a geek in the government… a guy (or gal) who gets to take billions — even trillions — of dollars when the urge strikes.

There is no winning a fight against a guy with a money press.

The solution…

Don't play the game.

Conservative investors are square in the Fed's crosshairs. These investors save their money (strike number one), buy fixed income investments (strike number two), and don't react to government intervention (strike number three you're out!).

So the Fed uses a combination of money creation, which drains value through depreciation of the currency, and financial repression, by artificially lowering interest rates to levels below inflation, to ensure losses for all but the longest or riskiest fixed-income buyer.

Between these two programs the Fed is able to comfortably take from conservative investors what they weren't willing to give up: their purchasing power. This power is handed to banks in the hopes that they'll lend it out, creating a multiplier effect in the economy.

Of course it's not working… but that's not the point.

The part of the program that IS working is the loss of value for conservative investors, which means they must find a different game.

If this particular investment path — traditional fixed income — is racking up losses through negative real interest rates (earning less than inflation), it's time to broaden your horizons a little. Don't think of it as fixed income investing. Think of it as a treasure hunt for yield.

For years we've prompted readers to search a little farther afield for yield. It can take many forms, well beyond the interest on a bond. Dividend stocks are a good starting point, but they're not for the faint of heart.

Yield is an area that has gotten a lot of interest in the past couple of years, so many people now fish in the same ponds. Regardless, the goal is to double-up, or to buy securities that have the opportunity for both capital gains in the Fed-driven market and the ability to pay cold, hard cash along the way.

If you can do that, then not only have you left behind a losing game of low yields on traditional fixed income, but you've also turned the Fed's game on its head. You can earn the return you want and still put the money in your account instead of spending it.

That sounds like winning to me.

CYCLES

Why There is Always a Boom and a Bust

January, 2013

Remember years ago when the markets were steady, the fundamentals were sound, and governments around the world weren't trying to manipulate the business cycle?

Me neither.

In fact, looking back through history it's difficult to pinpoint times when at least some of these things weren't going on and when the cycle of growth-mania-implosion-growth wasn't in play.

If we look across asset classes — stocks, bonds, metals, grains, energy and real estate — there is always one area that is zooming well beyond any reasonable valuation... only to soon be followed by a devastating crash.

If this is so common, and has been around since at least the Dutch Tulip mania and the John Law Mississippi Land Company, then the question becomes: "Why does it keep happening?"

Why do people, in the form of constituents, investors, savers and citizens, keep allowing markets and economies to zoom out of control?

The answer is" "We're all crazy."

Or at least, we're all irrational.

How else can we explain housing in 2005... the NASDAQ in 1999... gold in 1980... oil in 1979 and again in 2008... even bonds (and potentially stocks!) today?

In each case there's a situation — like the Iranian oil embargo, the Internet craze, wild credit lending and Fed intervention — that precipitates a market run, but people act as if it's normal... like it will continue forever.

And then it doesn't.

We know the cycle, we can cite numerous historical examples, and yet we fall for it over and over again.

We're crazy, right?!

Maybe, or maybe we're just human.

Part of the human make up is mental conditioning that gives our most recent experience the greatest weight in our judgment of what will happen… or should happen… in the future.

Think of all the people whose homes doubled in value from 2000 to 2005, but then "lost" half their value through 2010. On paper they're back to where they started… no harm, no foul. But in the minds of those people they're much poorer.

The same is true with income. If a person gets a raise from $80,000 in salary to $100,000, they feel great. If, a year later, that same person has to find a new job, but can only find one at $80,000, they feel undervalued.

In economic terms, Hyman Minsky played off of this mental conditioning to state that stability creates instability. His point was that when any market stabilizes, market participants begin to underappreciate risk. This lack of appreciation shows itself when people take on ever greater levels of risk in markets that have already made outsized gains.

Again, the housing market is a great example…

With valuations flying high in 2003-2004, well beyond traditional measures of affordability and long-term growth, it would seem obvious (in hindsight) that the market was ripe for a fall. Yet people kept buying. Why?

Well, every day they got up, looked at the world around them, and saw that prices had once again moved higher.

This brings back the old Groucho Marx question of: "Who are you going to believe, me or your own eyes?" A person could read about the perils of the housing market all day, or even hear the warning bells in his own head, but the prices on the ground kept moving higher. The risk seemed minimal indeed.

The interesting part is that there's so much written in defense of huge moves in markets. It's always the "new normal."

Gold was going not to $800, but $1,500, in 1980. Housing was going to remain at high levels and even move higher because of the stable interest-rate market and growing population. Oil was going to stay well above $125/barrel in 2008 because of Chinese demand.

There's always a reason for markets to remain at lofty levels, and even go higher. The thing is, they rarely do.

Unfortunately, it's the odd example of a permanent move that gives people some hope that this time really is different. For example, the oil embargo after the 1973 war in the Middle East permanently changed the structure of oil pricing.

Tectonic shifts like this are rare, even though people seem to see them in every market that is currently out of whack.

So when markets do finally break down, the fall is rarely gentle. Instead, prices and values come crashing to the ground as market participants all try to squeeze through the exit door at the same time, like all the depositors standing in the Bailey Savings and Loan in the movie "It's a Wonderful Life." It was a panic, and people were willing to sell their shares at a great discount simply to be out.

We see examples of booms and busts all around us, from idle container ships to natural gas fracking activities.

The forces that drive these trends reside in our heads.

As long as markets are made up of people, we can expect the boom and bust cycle to continue.

For us as investors, this is a wonderful thing!

Just think how boring it would be if all markets were calm and steady. There would be no advantage gained from analysis, as all risk/return would be equalized across asset classes. Everyone would have the exact same outcome along the continuum of risk… at which point, I suspect people would begin to make up risk just to relieve our minds from the monotony!

Luckily for us, we have plenty of markets out of whack right now to keep us occupied.

Off kilter markets, driven by outside forces or overly aggressive investment trends, are what we look for in our *Boom & Bust* portfolios. Whether we're on the long side of the trade, with infrastructure companies that pay handsome dividends, or on the short side, where we have a dim view of certain bond markets, the goal is the same.

We use our long-term economic research to inform our short-term analysis… looking for who's moving from growth to boom and who's about to go bust!

The Power of Routine

May, 2013

I stay away from giving parenting advice. Mostly I just tell stories of mishaps and upsets my own three kids create, while leaving the judgment calls to others.

But there is one thing I can tell any new parents that's helpful and non-judgmental. That is, create a routine.

Setting up an environment where kids know what to expect will reduce everyone's stress and allow the kids to grow up with fewer concerns. Schedule and communicate everything from meals, to bedtimes, to family time. Babies thrive on schedules, and older kids, even when they don't know it, use routines to build comfort zones.

But don't think routines are only good for kids...

My coffeemaker is set to brew at 4:50 a.m. I get up every weekday at 5:00 a.m. I sit down on the couch a few minutes after 5:00 a.m. and flip between the futures on CNBC and my local Fox station while I drink coffee and put on my running shoes.

I'm pretty predictable, to say the least, but that's okay. It gives me the structure I need to get my days off to the right start. I also like ordering the same meals at restaurants, but that's another story.

My point is that routines become ingrained in our lives and create comfort... as well as opportunity.

While each of us can have different routines in our personal lives, there are some bigger routines that create normal ebbs and flows for our society. Many of these routines are based on the calendar.

Think about shopping. We shop throughout the year for things like perishables. We even buy some durable goods and gadgets along the way. But most of our heavy duty shopping is reserved for the holiday season, which means there's an emphasis on retailers for the months of November, December, and January.

Then there's energy use. Americans love their cars and we drive endless miles. But the main concentration of our driving is during the summer months and, to a lesser extent, around Christmas.

In terms of home energy use, we heat our homes in the winte
up the A/C in the summer, with reliable breaks in the early fa'
spring. This creates down time for energy companies — particu.
early spring — when they can shut down some production and perform routine maintenance on their equipment.

These simple examples should seem so obvious as to make you think:
"So what?" There's a good reason I mention them. These are the exact types
of routines, or cycles, that Adam O'Dell uses in his *Cycle 9 Alert* service to
provide investors with an added advantage for creating gains in a difficult,
danger-filled market.

Instead of trying to tease out the newest tech winner, or figure out what
pharmaceutical company will win (or lose) FDA approval, Adam starts with
the common sense view that much of our economy moves in cycles that are
very predictable.

He breaks the investing world down into nine large sectors and then, using historical data, determines the short-to-medium-term cycles for each one.
From there, he uses baskets of securities to identify the top and bottom companies in each sector so he can pinpoint companies poised to gain — or lose
— big as the cycle starts.

This allows Adam to recommend when to get into a play and when to get
out, again for maximum gains as the sector moves through its natural cycle.

But Adam doesn't use Cycle 9 to recommend individual stocks. He knows
too much about our analysis at Dent Research to go down that road. (In fact,
he is the Portfolio Manager of our Boom & Bust portfolios where we hold
mostly income producing securities on the long side of the ledger while we're
short several investments as well.)

Instead, Adam uses options to gain exposure to the companies he believes
will make the biggest moves. If the company is expected to ride a cycle higher,
Adam recommends call options. If a cycle spells trouble for a company, Adam
will suggest a put option. Either way, your risk is simply the price of the option, which should be a fraction of what an investment in the company stock
would require.

If basing an investment strategy off of identifiable cycles and then using
options to limit your risk sounds like a good idea, that's because it is.

Since Adam's service went live in beta testing last fall, the results have been impressive.

This is a great way to augment your investment returns while we all wait out the craziness of the current Fed-fueled market.

WINTER SEASON

Is It Cold Enough for You?

July, 2012

The Summer Solstice, which marks the beginning of the summer season, passed not so long ago. I know because it falls on June 21-22, right next to a friend of mine's birthday.

This friend hates her birthday and always has.

Just imagine how interminable your birthday must seem when it falls on the longest day of the year. Never mind the record highs we're experiencing across the mid-west this season...

But my asking if it's cold enough for you has nothing to do with the annual calendar. Our focus is on the economy.

When things are hot in the economic world, it means there's a lot of growth and growing threat of inflation. If rising temperature is used as a metaphor for economic expansion, then the opposite should work also, where a stagnant or contracting economy can be described as stone cold.

That's why, I think the U.S. economy, and even the world economies, are encased in an iceberg. And the central banks of the world are attempting to melt this iceberg with a few blow torches.

Over two decades ago, Harry Dent identified the pattern of growth and contraction in developed, industrialized economies based on consumers. This pattern shows how the rise and fall of populations has a direct effect on economic activity and capital markets.

By looking at population charts, it is quickly discernible that populations tend to move in 40-year cycles, with two 40-year cycles (a surge in births and then a wave that meets the previous high) completing an 80-year loop.

The resultant economic trends occur in roughly 26- and 14-year waves with the first long wave going up and the second shorter wave moving lower. So in a complete 80-year loop there are two 40-year population waves (or generations), with two smaller waves inside... a 26-year wave up in spending and growth, and a 14-year wave down of saving and contraction.

Because people — even people like us — like to think of things in patterns, we identified the four "seasons" of the economy to correspond with the 26-14-26-14 pattern of a long 80-year economic cycle.

The first move up is 26 years of growth when a new generation has fully infiltrated into the workforce and begins spending more. This creates an economy that's warming and growing, just like spring.

The next phase is 14 years of summer, when things are hot, sticky and stifling… and the new generation is saving more.

Then comes the best season of all: fall. This is when the weather is fair, the summer harvest has been completed, and the fall harvest is coming in as well. There is plenty of everything to go around. Of course, all things must come to an end, which is why the next 14 years are like winter, with many things dying off and activity grinding to a halt again. The difficulties of winter make way for the new growth of spring and the cycle starts anew.

We're In the Winter Season

After 26 years of an economic Fall Season from 1982-2007, we're now five years* into the Economic Winter Season. That's why we've seen a lot of things change since the start of the credit crisis… and why we've seen economic activity drop dramatically.

Central banks have done their best to hold back the forces of economic "nature." Their weapon of choice has been stimulus programs. But it becomes clearer every day that these programs are about as effective as blow torches would be at melting away an iceberg. We need to go through the painful process of having many things "die" so that we can move on. That's the only way forward.

Currently the powers that be are keeping many institutions — from banks to whole countries — on life support by administering ever larger doses of financial drugs — bailouts and cheap loans. It won't work. These institutions are the walking dead, the last vestiges of the previous season that should be allowed to shake off their mortal coil to make way for the new growth the lies ahead.

Stopping the drug flow to the zombie banks and other institutions will return us to the natural business cycle without committing more capital (think about your tax dollars here) to a lost cause.

Of course, with the cold of winter there is little prospect for growth or inflation. That's why the *Boom & Bust* portfolio reflects an emphasis on income and short market positions, with a little long equity exposure as well. While we're always looking for good opportunities, we don't want to make the mistake of jumping into the markets just to be dragged down. This is like mistaking a warm winter day for the end of winter.

We have to recognize that even though things feel "warm" from time to time, this season has a long way to go.

Keep the coat and duck shoes handy.

* Now seven years.

CREATIVE DESTRUCTION

Out of a World of Creative Destruction Comes Innovation

January, 2013

At first the Energizer bunny ad theme was funny.

Then it was overdone.

Then it was incredibly annoying.

Just the sight of the little pink bunny with glasses and a bass drum can send people into a rage, all wishing for the chance to drop-kick the fuzzy ball of frustration into the next state.

At least on this front we now have some peace, but it comes with a cost. Energizer is steadily losing ground in the disposable battery business, which is causing the company to shut down plants and fire workers.

Welcome to the world of creative destruction, where innovation is painful… but helpful.

If you want to know the reason behind the decline in disposable battery sales, take a quick glance at almost any teenager. Handheld devices like PSPs and iPhones don't use disposable batteries. Neither do laptops or tablets.

As the mobile world converges to a few devices, the need for many different entertainment platforms — and their power supplies — is dwindling.

At the same time, the technology behind batteries themselves has evolved at a rapid pace, allowing rechargeable batteries to provide sufficient power for normal use.

For society, these developments bring great benefits.

As devices converge there should be a narrowing of what consumers want to own and carry, with only the software varying by user. And using rechargeable batteries lowers the amount of discarded disposable batteries that end up in landfills.

Other, larger benefits are only just beginning to emerge…

The additional resources being poured into small battery development for use in personal devices can lead to innovation in large battery technology. By "large" I don't mean like a car battery. I mean the suitcase-sized battery used in plug-in vehicles...

Even though there is a lot of hype around electric vehicles (EVs) today, the reality is that sales are slow and consumers are skeptical. For good reason. Right now plug-in cars (not hybrids) are severely limited in range because of their batteries.

The growth in EV use in California has been moderate, but is already causing problems as public charging stations in parking lots are full. If you drive an EV to the airport, counting on a charging station so you can make it home, you might be unpleasantly surprised. Greater range obviously helps to eliminate this issue.

Then there are storage-container-sized batteries used at electrical transfer stations...

This is where power generation and electrical use converge. Electrical use — meaning when consumers use their appliances, air conditioning, etc. — varies during the day, during the year and with the weather. Power generation can adjust to this use when using coal- or gas-fired plants because the energy company controls the input.

However, when green sources such as solar or wind are added to the mix, the timing of power generation becomes a question. If the wind is up there's no problem. If the wind dies down, end users face a real possibility of rolling blackouts during peak use hours.

This conundrum of not being able to match power generation from green sources with power use is one of the biggest hurdles for reliance on renewable energy. Having the ability to store large amounts of electricity in more efficient, deep cycle batteries is the missing link in the chain.

So while we worry over the loss of jobs as Energizer closes disposable battery plants, and we cheer the retirement of that dang bunny, it serves us well to remember that all of this is part of that vital economic process called creative destruction... where better, more efficient production and processes displace the old.

Along the way, that's how we raise our standards of living.

CHAPTER 3:
Employment

Remember the good old days when conversation about employment was boring? The government would release the unemployment rate — 6.2%, 5.3%, etc. — and that was it. Now... well... not so much. Not only do we have to look at the rate of unemployment, we have to figure out how many people are working part time and want a full time job, or how many people simply checked out and aren't looking at all.

The weak economy has persisted for so long that no one's really sure of what "full employment" looks like. Will older people stay at their jobs? Will young people move out of their parents' basements? Will the Bureau of Labor Statistics ever report a meaningful number that isn't gamed by odd adjustments like the "birth/death" adjustment? Who knows, but the topic is central to our economic health, so we must pay attention to it.

—Rodney Johnson

EMPLOYMENT

Jobs... What Jobs?

April, 2012

On Friday, April 6, 2012, the Bureau of Labor Statistics (BLS) reported that the economy had created 120,000 jobs in the month of March. This was more than 80,000 *less* than what analysts expected. In response, the financial markets around the world sold off, except the U.S. market. It was closed on Friday. But it caught up with the rest of the markets yesterday.

Okay, the jobs report was ugly. But I have a different question: Wasn't the "hope" of 205,000 jobs ugly as well?

To have people excited about an employment report that shows 200,000 new jobs is to have, basically, thrown in the towel.

In late 2008, our economy started shedding jobs. This we all know. It continued to shed jobs for two years. When the bloodshed finally ended, we'd added more than 10 million people to the rolls of the unemployed.

Now, typically after such a horrific economic period we'd get a fast and furious recovery.

Typically.

But this economy isn't typical, at least not in the sense most people use the word.

This recovery is not like the ones of the last several decades, which were all within an economic growth period (a period we call the Economic Fall Season). Instead, our latest slide and the ensuing recovery, if you want to call it that, are now firmly within the Economic Winter Season. This is a time when we spend less, we pay down debt, we save. This means we need fewer employees.

And it lasts for years.

As We Anticipated and Forecast

And this pattern is playing out just as we anticipated and forecast.

Our economy needs to generate roughly 125,000 to 150,000 jobs per month just to absorb the new additions to the workforce (kids coming out of school). That doesn't include the millions of people who were thrown to the unemployment line. To include them, we'd need to add 300,000 to 400,000 workers per month to make any meaningful headway in reducing unemployment.

Is that forecast anywhere? Absolutely not!

Instead, we have all sorts of tortured conversations going on about how "great" it is that we've seen around 200,000 jobs created per month for a couple of months. Now, as the latest unemployment results attest, reality has set in again.

This is why we have stuck to our guns about preparing and protecting our portfolios.

We get it. People "need" the stock markets to go up, so they try to put lipstick on the pig that is our economy. That doesn't mean it reflects reality.

As the truth of our economic situation comes back to hit people in the face, expect some very volatile markets and a lot of finger pointing. Also expect, eventually, for the Fed to come back to the pseudo-rescue with some new program.

Between now and then be glad there's a "bust" section in the Boom & Bust portfolio to protect what you've worked hard to build.

According to the Bureau of Labor Statistics (BLS)

November, 2012

I guess it wasn't enough to get all the benefits… now those 55 years and older are taking all the work as well!

The recent jobs figures came out the first week of November and there was a lot of back-slapping among politicians about how the economy is healing. With a whopping 170,000 new jobs created, things must be on an upswing.

Obviously I'm being sarcastic.

A mere 171,000 jobs created is barely enough to put all the new entrants into the labor force to work. But there is something worse than simply modest job growth going on.

Instead of seeing bright shining faces getting entry level jobs, the numbers reveal that positions are actually going to people who are nearing retirement…

According to the Bureau of Labor Statistics (BLS), of the 3.3 million jobs created since June of 2009 — the official end of the recession — the "55+ set" has captured 3.8 million jobs.

That's right. This group has taken more jobs than all of those created, which means the other groups combined had a net loss of jobs since the end of the recession.

That net loss is concentrated in one area. The 25-54 set lost almost 850,000 jobs in the same time period. The youngest group, 16-19, showed modest losses, while the 20-24 set showed modest gains. Essentially, those in their prime working years are falling behind while the grandmas and grandpas take home the paycheck.

Now, rather than simply thinking, "What a bummer" for all of those 25-54 year olds, think about what it means to the structure of our economy…

The greatest amount of household spending is done by those raising children and there's no doubt that most of this occurs in the age range of 25-54. If our economy has rotated to where employers are more likely to hire older people than the workers with families, then how will these parents have the means to spend?

The aging workers aren't going to spend us into recovery. They're going to pay down debts and save for retirement.

The economy must have the parents with kids at home blowing their pay-checks on guitar lessons, ballet and gymnastics, new shoes, designer jeans, iPads, and fast food.

Without this economic adrenaline, we're sunk. We might as well stay home and learn Japanese through Rosetta Stone, because we'll start to look like their economy very quickly.

Given that this is the current path, it bodes poorly for the year ahead. Don't expect mid-market retailers, those like J.C. Penney or others that focus on family spending to post stellar numbers. Along with that, it's likely that mid-market food retailers will also feel the pinch.

Of course, on the upside, chances are there's a little more room in the local ballet class if you're looking to get your kid into it.

Go ahead, you can ask Grandma to pay for it… she's the one with the job.

JOLTed Into the Current Reality

October, 2013

When I was a newly minted grad and working for a brokerage firm, everyone knew there was only one good way to get a decent raise…

Quit.

The logic went that your first employer, and maybe even your second, was more or less a training ground where you had the opportunity to prove your worth. As time went on you took your experience and leveraged it into a big, fat paycheck somewhere else.

From your first employer's point of view, they trained you. Sure, they might not have increased your pay as your skills grew, but that was alright because they took the chance on hiring you.

In the end, while the first company might have loved you, they were not going to bump your salary enough to keep you.

But the logic of all of this assumed one big thing…

…that there was another job available.

We never stopped to consider what would happen if there simply weren't any openings when shopping around to increase our income. Today, this is exactly what we find.

The Bureau of Labor Statistics (BLS) conducts a survey called Job Openings and Labor Turnover, or JOLT. This report shows the number of people quitting their jobs, the number of people fired, the number of people hired, and the total number of job openings. The intent is to get a deeper picture of the activity within the jobs market instead of simply totaling up the number of people working and not.

The BLS releases the report on a two-month lag so the latest data is from July. It shows that 2.3 million people voluntarily quit their jobs. That number, which is still more than 20% below the 2007 level, has remained steady for months. Layoffs have subsided, but job openings are not shooting higher.

Hmmm.

If fewer people are quitting and there hasn't been an increase in job openings, then clearly the labor market continues to offer very little opportunity to the unemployed or those new to the job market (recent graduates).

The unemployment report provides evidenced of this each month, showing that millions of Americans are still looking for work.

But this situation also reveals the dim reality for those who are employed. That is fewer of them have a chance of changing jobs.

Without this job mobility, or at least the threat of it, workers lose one of their main bargaining chips in negotiating pay and benefits. It's no longer a given that competent employees can find work somewhere else and get a pay raise to boot. It is entirely possible that somewhere else just doesn't exist today.

This lack of bargaining power leads to an obvious result: lower pay.

This doesn't mean employers go around cutting everyone's income, only that they're not driven to give substantial pay raises to retain employees.

The BLS JOLT report confirms some of what we, here at Dent Research, have been discussing for a long time. That is employment trends continue to work against workers, and probably will continue to do so for the rest of this decade.

The slowdown in turnover, along with the glacial pace of job creation, illustrates a labor market that is basically stuck in the mud.

While this might sound a bit gloomy for those not so thrilled with their day jobs, there is an opportunity here.

Instead of searching for other jobs that might not exist, employees can focus on cross-training, increasing their education, or even preparing to start their own business. Each of these activities can put a worker in a much better position when the economy — and the labor market — finally head higher.

Unemployment Stats Are Just Noise

October, 2013

Spit-balling employment used to be easy.

Just watch the tape at 8:30 a.m. eastern every Thursday morning (that's the release schedule for the U.S. Initial Jobless Claims) and you'd have a pretty good idea as to whether things were improving or not.

Not anymore.

The measure of new jobless claims in the U.S. economy represents people who are filing for unemployment benefits for the first time. Typically a number below 300,000 or so means there's a solid employment picture because few people are losing their jobs.

A number above 400,000 is something of a warning sign because obviously more people are losing work.

Unfortunately, there are two components missing here that can render this number next to useless...   *Unemployment - 278000 as of 1/20/15*

1) A reading between 300,000 and 400,000, and

2) A discussion about how many jobs are being created in the economy.

For about the past year, the jobless claims number hovered around 375,000 and has recently fallen to around 335,000. Some months it has been more, some months less. Unfortunately, a reading in the 300,000 to 400,000 range tells us absolutely nothing...

When Hurricane Sandy hit, the measure spiked above 420,000. Then, near the end of January the reading fell to 330,000. Both were outliers so they carried little weight. The four-week average is still sputtering, having declined slightly but still in no-man's land.

At the same time, the economy is not adding many jobs. There were net gains of around 200,000 jobs in November and December 2012, a net gain of 157,000 jobs in January 2013, and finally a gain of 236,000 jobs in February 2013.

There are roughly 150,000 new workers in the workforce each month. Adding barely more than enough jobs to absorb these new workers is not going to do much to alleviate the unemployment of millions of Americans.

Break this all down and it means one simple thing: Employment is still in the dumps. Yes, there have been signs that the labor market is no longer crumbling and that's good. But it's not the same thing as solid, steady growth.

This is what's so frustrating about reading the paper or listening to market pundits talk about jobless claims and even unemployment. They make it sound as if there's continual improvement when really we're simply treading water.

To create lasting growth in our economy, we need steady domestic demand. For that to happen, we need clarity when it comes to personal finances (taxes, health, energy, etc.). We need to reign in the wild debt-fueled spending of our government. We need the Federal Reserve to get out of the rate-setting business and the money-printing game.

Until those things happen, tepid demand will keep us in a pattern of tepid employment... and changes in statistics like U.S. jobless claims will simply be noise.

Keep an eye on them, but for now don't give them any power in influencing your financial or investing decisions.

So Where Do the Kids Go?

April, 2013

When they're young, Christmas comes slowly for kids. The days leading up to the holiday seem to drag on forever. The anticipation of the morning drives them mad. When the big day finally arrives, they wake up early and rip into their presents as though their lives depended on what secrets they unwrapped.

As kids get older, Christmas starts to show up — and pass — faster and faster. Instead, another day on the calendar becomes the one they count down to. It's a day that kids look forward to with more anticipation than all other days of the year combined...

The end of school.

It's the time of year when my kids can't seem to wake up with their alarm clock. Dinner table conversation centers around, "When will this end?!"... and the statement, "I am so done with school" has replaced the traditional "Hi, how was your day?" (and pretty much any other pleasantries).

But the days pass soon enough, and young kids all across the country are released from their own version of prison. And that's a problem...

Many young people spend their summers working, socking away money for college, saving up for a car, or generally replenishing their spending money. They take jobs that range from retail service to manual labor, generally on the lowest rung of the employment ladder.

Employers are glad to have the fresh faces show up because these workers are usually willing to accept very low wages and do jobs that others shun.

But that has changed.

This year* — like it has been for the last several years — when high school and college kids go in search of summer jobs, they'll find those positions already taken. The employment implosion of the last five years has led many who previously held middle income jobs to take anything they can find, which usually means positions typically held by the very young.

A great example of this is the position of stocker at major stores like Target. The job involves restocking shelves in the middle of the night or very early in the morning, while the store is closed. The work is part-time and pretty mindless so you can see why it appeals to kids. They can stay up all night, not put too much brain power into it, and still earn some money.

The same factors (except for earning money) that make it attractive to a 17-year-old are the factors that make it detestable work for those who need to support their families... yet they take the jobs anyway.

Because it's all they can find.

Our nation saw an uproar in 2009 and 2010 when unemployment benefits were extended to 99 weeks. Who needs unemployment for two years?

That was three years ago.

Unemployment is still high, and middle income jobs are the hardest to find.

The trickle down effects of this are clear. Those who used to hold middle income jobs are taking low income jobs. Their ability to earn and spend like they had in years past is severely curtailed. Their ability to grow in their career is also set back. Where do you go from part-time stocker?

Meanwhile, young kids looking for part-time work will find very few opportunities. So they'll spend more time on our couches at home, neither earning a wage nor getting valuable experience as an employee. The ramifications of this situation will be painful and with us for many years to come.

There is a bright spot though.

We're not Spain.

In Spain unemployment is 27.7%, with youth unemployment (people under 25) at 58%. Couches in Spain are getting crowded.

* 2013

Jobs at Any Cost... to Us

October, 2013

On a recent Sunday I was watching television, flipping between two programs. One was an NFL football game and the other was a C-Span broadcast of Dr. Doug Elmendorf's testimony before a House of Representatives panel.

I can't remember who won the football game, or even who was playing, but I found the U.S. House panel discussion riveting.

Such is the life of a data junkie.

Part of what struck me was Dr. Elmendorf's composure; part was sheer horror at the lack of economic understanding the representatives in attendance showed.

Dr. Elmendorf is the director of the Office of Management and Budget. He was there to discuss his office's recent report on the likely changes in our financial situation over the next several decades.

As usual, the politicians took very partisan views of the information and used their time to score talking points instead of delving further into the analysis.

The topics ranged from health care costs to Social Security payments, and often ended with statements that began with: "I'm sure my friends across the aisle…" What drivel!

But one line of questioning caught my attention. It was about the sequestered budget cuts and Dr. Elmendorf's estimate that the cuts will result in a loss of hundreds of thousands of jobs. The Congressman asking the questions was none other than my own Representative, Kathy Castor.

In her questions, Rep. Castor was genuinely interested in how the sequestered budget cuts would affect employment in general, and in her district specifically.

While Dr. Elmendorf couldn't address local affects, his analysis shows that the $85 billion in budget cuts will result in an estimated loss of 600,000 jobs.

Rep. Castor was very concerned. To her, this was an obvious reason to add the spending back to the budget. Clearly 600,000 jobs need to be preserved!

Or do they?

Since the game was on a commercial break and the testimony had moved on to another Representative asking silly questions, I did a little math...

Spending $85 billion for 600,000 jobs is the equivalent of $141,667 per job. An annual income at this level would put the worker in the top 10% of all earners in the U.S., which seems a bit excessive for government jobs.

But I don't think Rep. Castor ever stopped to do the math. I don't think her Legislative Aide for Economic Affairs did either. Instead, it appears that the mantra is: "Jobs at any cost!"

Do they ever think of who pays the cost?

As I've written previously, the Fed's followed this line of thinking for years, but it makes Congressmen look like kindergarteners.

While Congress wailed and screamed over $85 billion in budget cuts that span an entire year and put an estimated 600,000 jobs at risk, the Fed prints $85 billion a month in an effort to create jobs and only achieves the creation of about 175,000 of them.

Keep in mind, attributing the entire average monthly jobs gain of 175,000 to the Fed's efforts is being stunningly generous. Those gains are certainly not all because of the Fed's actions.

The Fed's efforts — in the best-case scenario — cost over $485,000 per job. This money, if it all flowed to the job holders, would put the workers not in just the top 10% of earners, but in the rarified air of the much-hated one-percenters.

Of course, there is slippage in both the Congressional and the Fed programs. While much of the money from Congressional cuts comes from workers, not all of it is salary and benefits. There are billions of dollars in capital expenditures and expenses for equipment, facilities, and other things that won't be made.

With the Fed, the connection to actual people is tenuous at best. There's no clear linkage to jobs other than a chain from the Fed to lower interest rates, which in turn fuels debt, which makes homes more affordable, so presumably more new homes are being constructed.

If we counted only jobs in sectors affected by housing, the number of jobs attributable to the Fed would be much lower.

No matter how the math works out in terms of jobs created through government spending or money printing, one thing is for sure: The person at the other end of the line, the one paying for all of this, is a particular sort of citizen.

They're a citizen who earns enough to pay federal income tax and who's managed to spend less than he earns over the years. In short, if you've worked hard to grow your income and have saved instead of spent every nickel, then Congress and the Fed have a continuing plan for you.

As long as their assessment of the employment market remains dim, they plan for you to fork over a bit more of your assets.

Part of the fight against this sort of thing is to lower your taxable footprint as much as possible. While there's not much you can do about earned income, there are certainly ways to position investments and holdings to bring down your tax bill.

Adding in some municipal bonds, either individually or in a unit investment trust, can do the trick while providing yield, particularly right now while tensions are running high over Detroit's bankruptcy. Tax planning with trusts can be very beneficial for those nearing or in retirement.

As for the Fed's printing, it's the only thing keeping the U.S. from its natural course of deflation.

Right now the dangerous game we all play is to stay invested in assets like equities, which are benefiting from the Fed's fight to re-inflate industries like housing. All the while we have to keep an eye on the exits for when the Fed's failures become widely recognized.

One thing is for sure... sitting around watching Congress and the Fed pursue jobs at any cost can be very expensive for the rest of us.

PART-TIME JOBS

Can You Answer This Word Problem?

October, 2013

Do you remember those word problems from Algebra?

"If a coffee seller has 300 pounds of coffee at $5 per pound, how many pounds of $9-per-pound coffee should he add so that his blend averages $6 per pound?"

That was the sort of thing I lived for in high school. A math problem wrapped up in words was right up my alley, which is probably how I got into this profession of writing about all things financial.

Over the years I came to realize that not everyone shares my love of such problems. In fact, many people run from them. However, I was not aware, until recently, that people bad at math are *also* writing about economics.

The trend in part-time jobs is a case in point.

Writers from *Bloomberg* to *Moody's* have been addressing the question of part-time job growth over the last month, pointing out that it's common for part-time jobs to flourish immediately after a recession.

This might be true, but for all of those going by establishment figures (which we don't), the recession formally ended in July of 2009.

That's not recent. In a business cycle, four years and three months is ancient history.

There is no way that our economy should be creating a bunch of part-time jobs right now. Instead, we should have had part-timers converting to full-time work more than two years ago, if we retraced what typically happens after a recession.

And how many of our recent jobs are part-time? "Not too many," these bad-at-math people claim. "Over the last year only three out of five new jobs created were part time," they say.

Hmmm.

The current employment structure of our economy has 20% part-time workers. Last time I checked, three out of five is 60%. This sets up a word problem from Algebra!

If your existing labor force is 20% part-time, and you add (a very questionable) 1.8 million jobs that are 60% part-time, is part-time employment in your labor force shrinking, growing, or remaining the same?

For those of you who hate word problems, I'll give you a hint: Our labor force is quickly adding low-paying, low-skilled, part-time jobs that are diluting the existing structure of employment.

While we're not a part-time nation by any stretch of the imagination, adding more such jobs — particularly four years after the recession officially ended — is a travesty.

We keep talking about such points to highlight the lack of progress in our economy. It's not that we delight in this sort of thing. We want people to be very clear, not only about the current state of the nation, but also about what lies ahead.

If a majority of the jobs we're creating are part-time, then how are the workers in those jobs supposed to support their families?

Or pay taxes?

Or grow their savings?

The slowly changing nature of our economy today has very long-term implications for the structure of our nation tomorrow.

We would all do well to take a minute and consider another, yet related, word problem:

If millions of young people join the economy and can't earn enough income to support themselves, how will they contribute to support the wellbeing of the millions of boomers as they retire in the years to come?

CHAPTER 4:
Demographics

I think in the dictionary under "boring" is the definition — demographics. It's hard to imagine a less emotional word, one that conveys less meaning or gives rise to less visualization. As an exercise, say the word demographics out loud and see what comes to mind. My guess is… nothing. That's unfortunate, because while the word seems stale and lifeless, under the surface it's a bundle of activity. People are dying, babies are born, immigrants move, money is spent, college is attended, taxes are levied, and so on.

Trends in populations drive the world. It's that simple.

From the meteoric rise of China as its population urbanized to the withering of Japan as its population dies off, the changes brought about by trends among populations are clear. While such things don't change course day to day, we must give them the proper place of importance when analyzing other data in our decision making.

—Rodney Johnson

SPENDING WAVE

How a Conversation About Washing Machines Affects Your Investments

March, 2012

The other day I found myself talking to a few other parents about washing machines.

The notion that a washing machine now costs nearly $1,000 seems ridiculous to me. And the idea that someone would pay $200 for the stand to put the washing machine on is just icing on the cake. A stand doesn't make the washing capacity bigger. It doesn't make the unit more efficient or reduce energy or water consumption. The capability to handle different types of fabrics also has nothing to do with the pedestal.

Then it hit me: "I'm having a lucid, multi-point conversation about washing machines."

Self-loathing *almost* describes how I felt at that moment. No matter how you spin it (no pun intended), there's nothing cool about gabbing up the latest and greatest in clothing care. I'm old. Or more to the point, I'm at the stage of life where this sort of thing matters. It's natural, no matter how uncool it is.

And that is what makes our economic world go round (again, no pun intended).

When Being Average Matters

As a guy in his mid-40s with a lovely wife and three teens, I'm smack in the middle of the averages as far as Americans go. I got married in my mid-20s, started having children a few years later, and all along the way I pushed my spending higher... doing what I can to maintain and then increase our standard of living.

While not everyone follows this path, the overwhelming number of Americans (and members of other developed populations) do this exact thing — get married, have children, and match their spending to their current stage of life.

There's nothing magical about this. When you add more people to the household, you spend more money.

These are people you presumably care about, so you'd be willing to go the extra mile for them. The older they get, typically the more expensive they are to maintain. Just think about how much food a 17-year old puts away or, I shudder to consider it, the cost of car insurance for a teenager.

I have two teenage drivers. My annual car insurance is enough to buy a modest used car every year!

There is no question the expense of raising children goes up as they get older. As parents, we foot the bill.

Then we get the mother of all bills — college. This is kind of the grand finale of spending. But even without this blowout expense, children are the most expensive to their parents in their last years at home.

Now, today's issue isn't a rant against, or even about, the cost of children. Instead, it's to illustrate that people go through different stages of life in waves.

Over the past thirty years we saw baby boomers, the largest group in our population, go from pot-smoking, smelly hippies to BMW-driving yuppies and then to sometimes indulgent, overbearing parents. The transition brought with it waves of spending that drove our economy higher.

Even though wages remained flat, this spending pattern occurred through the use of massive amounts of debt, from credit cards to home equity lines of credit (HELOCS).

But this wave of boomers' spending more has crested. We reached the top when the highest number of Boomers, those born in 1961, reached their peak spending year in 2009.

The trend lower, that we're in now, is just as obvious and apparent as the trend higher was during the '80s, '90s and even part of the 2000s.

Today, the bulk of baby boomers aren't focused on raising children. Their kids are out of the house. Instead, today, the talk is all about paying down debt and saving for retirement.

These are not activities that drive our economy higher. They're activities that will lead our economy to shrink, which is why we have forecast a long, difficult economy ahead.

The Power of the Spending Wave

To put this information in graphic form, we developed the Spending Wave. It tracks people in the U.S. by their peak spending years. Notice the peak in 2009 is followed by a sharp drop and, after a few twists and turns. It takes until the early 2020s before we see a significant rise.

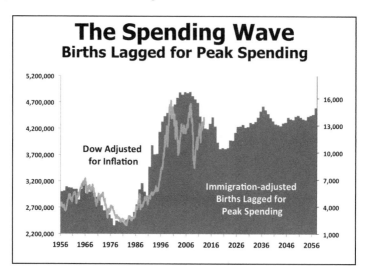

Notice what's missing here: There is NO reference to the Fed... or a politician... or any outside force. That's because consumers don't consult politicians before they spend money on their families or save money for retirement.

With that being the case, don't expect any policy out of the Fed or Washington to "fix" our situation. It takes time. Time (in fact almost a decade) for the next group in our economy to have kids and start spending with abandon.

DEMOGRAPHICS

Expect to See More Irish Bars

January, 2014

I used to go to Jazz Fest in New Orleans every year with a group of old friends. We'd all gone to high school in the area, and then off to different colleges, so this was our annual get together.

As usual, when we finished the night in the vicinity of Bourbon Street, we'd find ourselves in the Irish Pub. We'd sing the Irish drinking songs with gusto, filling ourselves with Harp, Guinness, and Jameson.

On the way home one year it struck me that it was odd to find such a great Irish bar in New Orleans... a town of decidedly French descent. Then I realized! There seems to be a great Irish bar in EVERY town I've ever lived in and most towns that I've visited.

Now, after years of demographic study, I think I know why...

The Irish leave their homeland at one of the fastest rates in the world, and then spend the rest of their lives pining for it. This drives them to open bars in whatever town they find themselves, serving Irish beer and whiskey while paying like-minded, depressed Irishmen to sing ballads. The rest of us are just along for the ride!

Given that widespread emigration is once again a fact of life for the Irish, we can expect to see more Irish bars popping up in cities around the world.

Over the last four years the Irish government estimates that roughly 400,000 of its countrymen have left the nation. The population of the tiny state is only 4.5 million, so this is a loss of almost 10% of its people, which would be like the U.S. experiencing an exodus of 30 million.

Keep in mind that the drain isn't constant across age groups. Those who leave are mostly of working age, with half of them less than 25 years old and half of them between 25 and 44.

This trend drains the country of the exact people who would typically be working, paying taxes, and growing their spending. In short, it hollows out the economy. But, for the Irish, this isn't their first go-round.

The Irish Potato Famine is probably the best known instance of mass exodus from Ireland. More than one million people died, and another million left the nation for other shores. At the time, this reduced the nation's population by more than 20%.

Ireland experienced another tremendous emigration surge in the late 1980s, which lasted until 1995, losing tens of thousands of able-bodied workers in most years. The drain of manpower and families robbed the nation of its natural fuel for growth.

This situation turned around in the late 1990s when the Celtic Tiger was unleashed, drawing tens of thousands of displaced Irishmen back home, as well as attracting immigrants from other countries. Unfortunately, it turned out to be a paper tiger, cut from the cloth of financial innovation and banking shenanigans that eventually fell apart.

The remnants of the crisis left many jobless and penniless, and the austerity imposed by the Troika — the European Central Bank, the European Commission, and the International Monetary Fund — has greatly reduced wages, public spending and pensions. So the Irish leave home, looking for better opportunities. And they open bars.

Interestingly, the Irish leave home at the fastest rate of any country in Europe, including Greece!

Luckily for the Irish, their tax laws are unique, allowing big companies like Apple to set up shop and avoid billions of dollars in taxes. This is a draw for international corporations, which do create some employment opportunities in the largest metropolitan areas.

At the same time, the Irish are very un-European in their view of family life. While their rate of child bearing (2.01 per woman of child-bearing age) is just below the rate needed for population replacement, it's far ahead of most European nations.

That means that as the Irish situation improves... and then deteriorates again... there should be enough of the countrymen to keep opening bars in far-flung places for decades to come! That's good news for the rest of us.

For the meantime, this situation points out the continued hardships in the countries of Europe that were hard hit in the downturn, and the fact that the PIIGS (Portugal, Ireland, Italy, Greece, and Spain) have not yet recovered.

For those looking for a place to invest in 2014, I'd suggest that, when it comes to Ireland, its beer is a better bet than its stock market.

What is It About Golf?

September, 2013

Jack, my golf pro, must be dead by now. He was in terrible shape 25 years ago when he gave me lessons.

I was a college graduate and had just received a pair of golf shoes, a five iron and a set of lessons as graduation presents. My father believed that playing golf went hand-in-hand with business success.

Unfortunately Jack really liked smoking cigarettes, so he wheezed, coughed and hunched. This rail-thin man would ride from the club house to the practice range, a distance of about 100 feet, and sit in the cart while I flailed about.

In my first round of golf, I got a birdie. Golfers will recognize this term as a score of one less than the expected number of strokes required to play a hole. But that's not the kind of birdie I got. Instead, one of my tee shots was a line drive about a foot off the ground (a bad shot, certainly) that actually killed a bird.

Even though my golfing career got off to a rough start, I really enjoyed it. There was the fresh air, the openness, the chance to compete against myself for improvement, and the constant need for attention to detail that makes the game so compelling.

But I don't play anymore. I've played one round in eight years. I just don't have the time. It's as if my life and golf are incompatible, and I'm not alone...

The National Golf Foundation (NGF) reports that from 2005 through 2010 the sport lost a net four million players, and currently golf participation is at its lowest level in more than 25 years.

Keep in mind that during the last 10 years this drop in golfing has occurred while the population of those at the prime age for the sport — empty nesters and young retirees — has been growing.

The NGF and other golf associations are desperate to turn the tide, but aren't sure how. Some information in their survey reveals the problem, but probably not in the way the associations think.

When those who are interested in golf, but don't currently play, were asked why they weren't taking to the greens, the number one answer was: "My spouse/significant other doesn't play."

Using this as a starting point, many in the game have begun championing programs that foster player development, women's groups, family outings and other ways to include entire families or couples.

On the surface this makes sense, but it brings up questions. Were there a bunch of spouses playing golf in the previous generation? Did women suddenly opt out of the sport and thereby pull their husbands with them?

I doubt it.

I think the problem with golf is much more about my father's point of view — that golf goes hand in hand with business success — than that of my wife's.

While it's true that my wife doesn't play the game, it's not true that I need to pursue the game for business development or contacts. From the outside looking in, it appears that golf has lost its position as a common meeting place for potential business associates.

Those left playing the game are the ones who truly enjoy the sport and make the time to play, not the ones who are marginally attached as they look for another networking opportunity or the chance to rub elbows with the boss.

If my view is correct, then it means golfing associations are struggling with the wrong questions. They're working very hard to make golf a faster game by changing the number of holes in a round… they're revamping their offerings to include more inviting lessons and player development for spouses and families.

Yet it's entirely possible that the sport should instead be considering how many golfers are left once the possibility of drumming up business is removed, or at least greatly diminished, and what lies ahead as our nation ages.

By focusing on changes in the game rather than on the reason people play, these associations could be damaging their own growth in the years ahead.

For the next 30 years, America will get older as baby boomers move through the empty nester and retirement phases of life. This should be a good time for the game of golf as more boomers retire because there'll be increasing numbers of potential players who now have the leisure to play if they so choose.

But what happens when these potential players get to the course and there are a bunch of small kids running around and groups of beginners clogging the practice range and the fairways? Or when those who return to golf are told that on Tuesdays and Wednesdays the course only allows for rounds of 12 holes?

This strikes me as being similar to the ill-fated advertising of Las Vegas in the early 1990s when the city tried to make itself a family-friendly place. Really?!

It failed miserably, and the town didn't shoot to the moon until it embraced its racy side with the highly successful "what happens in Vegas stays in Vegas" campaign. Basically it went back to its roots.

Golf should do the same. Be a refuge for people who enjoy the elitist edge of the game, who enjoy walking around in funny clothes and cursing a little white ball. There should be more than enough people in the years to come who want to be in the clubhouse to put golf back on a growth trajectory.

STATISTICS

What I Learned From Dead People

May, 2013

No, I'm not channeling the movie *The Sixth Sense*. I don't see or hear dead people… but I do learn from them.

In this case, it's regarding the oft-quoted statistic that life expectancy has increased by thirty years since 1900. Back then, people lived to the age of 48. Today they're living to the ripe old age of 78.

That's weird, don't you think?

That figure implies that in 1900 there were no "old" people, or that old was anyone near 50. No gray haired people? No 70-year-old grandparents kicking around?

That doesn't make sense.

So I checked into it…

Sure enough, the average age of death for a man in 1900 was 48. The average age of death for a man today is just over 78. That is indeed a 30-year difference.

HOWEVER…

If I look at the rate of death by age, the numbers get skewed.

Yes, the average age of death in 1900 was 48, BUT over 15% of the deaths occurred before the age of five.

This enormous number of deaths before the age of five had the effect of dramatically lowering the average age of death in those days. For many of those who made it past five years old, they survived well into their 70s and 80s, which is much closer to what we'd expect, given our knowledge of relatives and people at the time.

Interestingly, we commonly attribute the extension of life to advances in health science that allow us to live into old age. The reality is that advances in health science stopped us from dying as children.

This is yet another example of misleading averages. When you dig just a little deeper it's immediately obvious that the average age of death in 1900 is a pretty useless number. The same thing happens in the world of investing…

Since 1926, the average return on large cap stocks has been around 9%. That seems pretty good. I'd like a 9% return each year.

But of course the return is not 9% every year, it's just the average. In fact, the returns are quite spread out. Technically speaking, the returns have a wide dispersion from the mean. So if the average return is 9%, but there's a wide dispersion from this number, then how do we know what to expect each year?

Good question.

Most, if not all, financial software uses normal distributions and standard deviations to calculate expected returns for investments. Without getting too complicated, the software assumes that the returns are normally distributed (like a bell curve), with a set standard deviation (or how far each year strays from the expectation of the average).

So the average return of large cap stocks may be 9%, but the standard deviation is 19%.

To be 99% sure that your estimate of next year's return is correct, you must be willing to accept a range of returns. In this case, that range is three standard deviations above and below the average of 9%.

You read that correctly.

To be 99% sure — not 100%, mind you — that you have a good estimate of next year's return on large cap stocks, you must be willing to accept a range of returns from 9% minus 57% (three standard deviations below) to 9% plus 57% (three standard deviations above). In other words, a range of negative 48% to positive 66%, or a 114% spread around the expectation of 9%!

What kind of planning is that?!

Who in their right mind would invest in something with the thought that it's "okay" to have anywhere from a loss of almost 50% to a gain of more than 60% each year?

That's crazy!

And yet that's the exact way most financial software operates.

If you suddenly feel less sure about buying and holding equities, and have less faith in the statement that "over the long term, equities go up," join the club!

There are better ways.

Instead of simply plodding along, buying and holding with the hope that it all works out in the end, be proactive!

Take an active role in estimating the risk and reward potential of markets, industries, and individual securities.

Look across the economic landscape at the different forces that are driving markets at the moment and ask yourself: "Does all this make sense?" If the answer is "No," then you could be set to experience the low end of the expectation range for equities!

INTERNATIONAL VIEW

The Incredible, Shrinking... Powerhouse?

January, 2014

Over the past five years, Germany has done something amazing: It has maintained economic dominance in the face of daunting hurdles that have impeded the growth of surrounding countries.

It's done this largely by relying heavily on exports.

But along the way, Germany started taking heat from the leaders of other countries — including the United States — because they believe that Germans aren't doing their fair share of spending.

The theory is that the Germans are pretty good at making stuff other people want to buy, like cars, but they aren't putting enough of their revenues back into the world economy through consumption. If the German people would only spend more, then they would boost the economic fortunes of neighboring nations and thereby assist in the recovery of the European Union.

So far, the German people haven't taken the bait, and I don't expect them to anytime soon. Not because they don't understand the situation or don't want to consume, but because they recognize their own, individual circumstances.

That is: Germany is shrinking... at least in terms of people.

The German population had a mild baby boom at the same time the U.S. and most other Western nations did, creating a bump in the number of people born from the late 1940s through the early 1960s.

However, Germany didn't have a significant echo boom, or surge in births, during the 1980s through the 2000s, like the rest of us. This has left its population with more old people than young people... a lot more.

As of 2013, only 13% of Germans were less than 15 years old, while 21% were over 65. The situation is the same in Japan. The 66% in the middle are skewed toward the older ages. This shows that that the German birth rate is exceptionally low — hovering around 1.4 children per woman of child-bearing age — and has been for more than a decade.

In short, the Germans aren't having enough children to replace their existing population, much less grow.

Last year, the German census reported that its population had shrunk by 1.5 million people. Current estimates suggest that the country could lose an additional 20% of its population, or 19 million people, by the year 2060.

An aging, shrinking population is *not* a good thing. It takes a toll on government-provided services, like pensions and health care, and strains the labor force by starving it of incoming workers. It also creates a weird vortex in consumer spending.

As people age, they tend to spend less as they focus on saving for retirement. This is exactly why current pressure to force the German people to spend more won't work. They don't *want* to spend more.

The bulk of them are past their peak in spending and are much more concerned about making their money last through retirement than spending more today just to assist in the recovery of the spendthrifts Spain and Greece.

In order for the German population to increase its spending, there would have to be a dramatic increase in the number of young people in the economy, with economic wants and needs that come with going through the early years of adulthood.

Since the birth rate in Germany continues to hover around exceptional lows, this won't happen anytime soon.

The aging of the populations in Northern Europe, specifically Germany, is one of the main reasons there won't be a significant economic rebound in the region for years to come.

While the U.S. is still treading water economically, at least we have the horsepower necessary to eventually pull out of our slump because, relatively speaking, we have lots of kids.

While this is a conversation about a Northern European country instead of one of the Club Med nations, the end note is the same: There won't be a broad economic recovery in the euro zone anytime soon. The Southern states don't have any money to spend as they focus on paying down debts, and this very powerful Northern state has no interest in spending.

Expect the euro to come back down in the months ahead as this realization sinks in.

The Country That Will Outgrow Every Other

April, 2012

"Scotty, we need more power!"

"Dang it Captain, I'm giving it all she's got!"

This infamous exchange on the USS Enterprise is a particularly apt analogy for what's happening in India today.

India recently saw a dramatic reduction in its GDP growth from 10% to 7%.

India is the 10th largest economy on the planet. Over the last ten years, its exports have grown steadily and now stand at 18% of GDP. The country provides agricultural, chemical and manufactured goods. It has a significant service industry. It's a major player in the rapidly growing medical tourism sector.

So why the sudden, sharp, decline in GDP growth? The answer lies in power... or rather, the lack thereof.

Heavy-Handed Government Policies
Slow the Indian Powerhouse

As a carryover from its old Soviet-style of management, the Indian government sets rates on many essential items, including power. Currently, the government requires coal miners to sell their product 70% below market prices. This acts as a natural restraint on production because Indian miners would literally go broke providing coal at that rate.

So, the electric plants that rely on coal (which is most of them in India) are now faced with shortages. This results in blackouts, which cut industrial production.

The New York Times reported that demand for power now outstrips the supply of power by over 10%.

Imagine what this situation must be like. Your business has enough orders to keep your factory humming along at full capacity, but you can only run at 90% because you lose electricity for several hours every day.

Well, this is *exactly* what's happening in India. And it's creating a catch-22 situation...

Without Power, India Can't Increase its Power Capacity

A country can't build power plants unless the operators can prove they have a coal supplier. For this, they need a written supply contract, which is proving nearly impossible to get thanks to the government's ridiculous 70%-below-market rates on coal supply.

Without a written supply contract, ground never gets broken to build the plant. All the while, businesses in the country continue to expand and millions of poor Indians continue to flood into the cities for work, pushing the teetering infrastructure to the brink.

The solution here is clear: India will embrace alternative sources of energy for electrical generation, like natural gas. It'll also eventually deal with the bureaucratic road blocks to growth.

It has no choice, with a population of more than 1.1 billion and demographic and consumer spending waves working in its favor. Its working-age adults are young, hungry and they're entering their peak-spending phase. More than a third of the country's population is moving into the cities, where they're earning more. This is something the Indian government simply can't ignore.

However, the country has been independent for less than a century. It has been working on free market reforms for just a few decades. We must accept that there will be growing pains. The power problem is an example.

Despite that, with the demographic trends India has in its favor, it will eventually outgrow every other country for the next 25 years, which is why we have our eye on it.

As soon as we see the Indian government streamline the regulatory environment, so that business owners can get back to business, we'll position ourselves for the inevitable boom.

400 Billion People... Gone

May, 2012

How often have you heard, "Nothing moves in a straight line?" This is a common statement from market pundits, teachers and parents. But when it comes to talking about populations, the assumption has always been that we move in a straight line... up.

This is *not* our view. It *never* has been. We've pointed out time and again that populations move in waves. Through the '50s, '60s and early '70s, the world was on a wave up. Since then we've been on the down side of the wave.

Unfortunately, most people only remember and talk about the *Population Time Bomb*, as penned by Paul Erlich, or other tomes that discuss the Malthusian idea of too many mouths to feed.

Here's a new one for you: The most populated country on the planet — China — is on the verge of a population decline. It will follow in the footsteps of Japan and most of Western Europe. It, and many other countries, has chosen to bend the demographic curve.

In the process, they'll all bend their economies... and not in a good way...

Japan is the best example of what happens when you bend the demographic curve.

The country experienced a meteoric rise in the '60s and '70s, and then went supernova in the 1980s. Its fall from grace in the 1990s and 2000s is well documented. What is not discussed often enough is the country's lack of families and the role that plays in its continued economic woes.

In Japan, the birthrate among women of child-bearing age is roughly 1.28. This means each woman has, on average, just over one child. That child might replace her, but it doesn't replace her husband. So Japan's population is declining.

The last estimate I saw was that one-third of the Japanese population will simply disappear by 2050 because a quarter of the population is older than 65 and the young are not having kids. This is going on in what was the second largest economy on the planet, a status that China has now taken over as Japan has suffered not one but two lost decades.

But here's the kicker — China is also set for a population bust, one it brought on itself with the force of law.

China Cut off its Nose to Spite its Face

Back in the early '80s China was in a sad state. The country needed to modernize, but it was mired in a baby boom that left it scrambling to simply feed its population, much less educate them and grow productivity. So, the government implemented its infamous one-child policy that limits urban families to one child and rural families to two children.

In the ensuing decades, China has reduced its population burden by 400 billion people. Of course, at the same time, the country has urbanized and industrialized, so now families are used to being small.

Now China is facing the reality that its population is set to fall — *fall* — in the years ahead. If China's birth rate picks up from its anemic 1.58 children per woman of child-bearing age to 2.1 (the replacement rate), it might — just might — have a small decline in population by 2050.

But if China sees no increase in child births, which is much more likely, then it's possible this country of 1.3 billion could see a decline of 300 million people in the next 50 years. This is the same as losing the entire population of the U.S.

The problem with China is that the country is growing old — fewer children are being born and the current population is aging — before it grows rich. There isn't a large pot of gold at the end of a retirement rainbow just waiting to pay benefits to all of the retiring Chinese. There aren't enough young workers to pay taxes at a rate that would support those retiring.

What's a government to do? This is where things get dicey.

While the bending of the demographic curve might be great for the planet, it will mean serious adjustments for those looking to receive benefits in shrinking countries.

For now, Obama may wish he was presiding over the Chinese economy, but 50 years from now, he'll be glad he won't need to rely on the central government to determine his quality of life or help fund his retirement.

That makes two of us.

Trading Kids for Cash

January, 2013

No, this isn't about kidnapping, human trafficking, or anything so horrific. This is about a much larger demographic trends... one with much greater (although less sinister and appalling) consequences.

Potential parents are opting out.

For years we have written about demographic trends, a really boring word that addresses the even more boring practice of counting people and listing their attributes.

Blah.

The reason we can do this every day without shooting ourselves is because the outcome of the analysis is so fascinating and important. Demographics might sound boring, but the demographic trends are big enough to cause entire countries to rise and fall.

And right now, there's a high-flier country shaking with fear...

South Koreans look down the road and see... nothing.

World War II left Korea split after the Japanese were kicked out, with the North run by a Russian-installed dictator and the South run by a U.S.-installed dictator.

The North attacked the South to start the Korean War, which is what drew the Americans into the conflict.

In the aftermath of that war, the U.S. became intent on building the small nation of South Korea into a democracy with a vibrant economy. For the first 10 years the U.S. was responsible for 90% of South Korea's GDP.

The strategy worked and the country moved through the stages of economic growth at light speed. Its main lines of GDP moved from farming to heavy industry, then to light industry and finally precision manufacturing, all within 50 years.

At the same time, the country's politics moved from a combination command-economy and oligarchy to a true democracy, where it stands today.

The pace of change was phenomenal, and has brought the South Koreans to the point of being one of the most sophisticated and well-educated populations on the planet.

And that's where the trouble lies.

As populations move from villages and farming to urban settings with factories and production jobs, the traditional need for more children disappears.

More hands make light work on a farm but city dwellers know that more mouths to feed simply divides a small pie even further. In economic terms, kids are a drag. The greater the wealth and urbanization of a nation, the lower their child-birth numbers tend to be.

This is in evidence all around the world, with some notable exceptions like the U.S. Here at home our consistently (and only relatively) high birth rate is due more to recent immigrants having lots of children than because the domestic population continues to grow.

But back to South Korea...

Part of the reason for fewer children in developed countries is that the continued pursuit of a knowledge-based economy in concentrated areas is so expensive. The cost of living in a large city, paying for housing, food, medical care, and education is overwhelming. And this doesn't include preparing for one's own retirement.

Every child added to that situation compounds the cost because they have their own set of needs to address.

South Korea, with its high-tech, silicon-wafer corridor, rising auto manufacturing star companies, and its status as the most wired (by Internet connectivity) country on the planet, has shot past the point where having more children is a blessing.

Parents, or prospective parents, are finding the cost of raising just one child a heavy burden. So they're making the economic choice to have fewer kids, if any at all.

The result is South Korea now has fewer children per woman of child bearing age than any other country.

By this measure, each woman needs to have 2.1 children — to replace herself and her husband, plus a little for mortality — simply to keep the population from shrinking. Right now South Korean women of child bearing age are having 1.2 kids on average... that's almost half the number required to just keep the population constant!

And it's below Japan, which ties with Italy, and surprisingly Germany, at about 1.3. It's also below China, which clocks in around 1.5. All of these countries are moving toward self-selected extinction, but South Korea is moving the fastest!

In the short run, this means nothing. South Koreans will still wake up tomorrow morning and go to work. Their banks will still function and their factories will still run.

But in the long run, this means everything.

South Korea is sprinting to where Japan sits today — a rapidly aging country with sky-rocketing entitlement costs and a shrinking labor force.

The effects on Japan are clear. The country is desperately fending off continued deflation. Its national finances are in shambles as the government debt-to-GDP sits above 230%.

Sure, the country is still home to some of the best companies in the world, like Toyota and Honda, but one has to wonder how long these companies will stay there. At some point, the country will be one massive sale of assets. It's not really a question of "if" anymore, but when.

So the South Koreans are near the front of the line in making a decision on how to address an aging, developed society… and there are no rules.

The Japanese are widely seen as having done it wrong. They hate immigration and keep their work rules rigid. Any attempts to break open their job market have been crushed by older workers still benefiting from the current system. But it's like protecting one's seat at the Captain's table on the Titanic.

For us, watching South Korea move to such an extremely low level of child births is a flag of caution about investing in the country. Just as Japan's low birth trend has led to decades of deflation and a cratering stock market that is now stagnant at low levels, South Korea could follow the same path.

If you're adamant about investing there, look to the large exporters… and above all else, watch those investments carefully.

BRICs

Hit by a BRIC(K)

August, 2013

There are many different one-liner jokes in the world, including the series that starts with: "You know you're in trouble when…"

You know you're in trouble when the captain of your cruise ship runs toward the railing in a life vest.

You know you're in trouble when your accountant's resignation letter was postmarked in Zurich.

Now we can add one from the world of finance: You know you're in trouble when Greece outpaces your stock market.

From the end of 2012 through the middle of August, all four BRIC countries could claim this dubious distinction. In U.S. dollar terms, Brazil's stock market was down 29.9%, Russia's market was down 14%, India's market had fallen 21.4%, and China's market had dropped 7.1%.

During that same period, the Greek stock market had posted a 1% return.

Of course, it is possible the Greek market is simply at a standstill, providing no gain or loss because the country is in a deep freeze, but we'll leave that line of thought for another day. The point here is all about the BRICs… and how they've fallen.

In large part, global consumption drove the incredible growth in these four countries — along with many others around the globe — over the past fifteen years. The thirst for energy and gadgets exploded during the late 1990s and early 2000s, giving raw material providers and cheap labor countries an incredible boost to their economies and their markets.

Yes, the 2008 financial crisis briefly hit these providers, but then the central banks of the world took over.

As they flooded the world with cheap capital, providers of raw materials and cheap labor got their second wind. It seemed for a couple of years — from 2009 through 2011 — that these countries would be able to take a pass on the fallout from the greatest financial upheaval since the 1930s.

Until now.

As a bubble in debt and asset prices in emerging markets replaced the one in the developed world, everyone exhaled a collective sigh of relief. The feeling was that a rise of economic activity in these young, developing nations could offset a drop in activity in the aging countries of the world. This view held for a while, then reality snuck in the door.

It turns out that, while these youthful economies do have legitimate domestic consumption and growth, most of their outsized gains are reliant on selling to those stodgy, old, Western economies — as well as Japan — that are now in a funk.

Without the U.S., the European Community, and Japan buying more and more, the BRICs had to devise their own plan for creating growth, which typically involved extending a lot of credit on easy terms. We all know how this story ends — with lots of bad loans and questionable assets on bank books.

The last six months have been something of a wakeup call, with many previously high-flying countries that rely on exporting to either the EU or the U.S. — or their suppliers — pushed back on their heels.

In U.S. dollar terms, South Korea is down over 10%, Mexico has dropped more than 6%, and even Canada, which is not a young country but is definitely a raw materials supplier, has fallen by 3.6%. In fairness to our neighbor to the north, their stock index is up 1.1%, but adjusted for currency movement the return is -3.6% in U.S. dollar terms.

As we move into the fall of 2013 and turn the calendar to 2014, we expect this trend to continue.

Economic activity in the U.S. is steady, at a very low level. There are no signs of a robust explosion to the upside. Likewise, Europe isn't spiraling down, but it's not on a soaring trajectory either. This leaves the BRIC economies and their compatriots to deal with growth internally... and now to deal with their own mini-credit bubbles and locally inflated asset prices.

In addition to taking a backseat to Greece when it comes to market returns, it's possible that one of these countries or a group of them could trigger the next global financial crisis... and that's no joke.

STUDENT LOANS AND DEBT

Haley's Parents Should Have Listened to Us

March, 2013

In 2011 our family dog, Scout, died. Scout had been with us for over a decade, the product of a trip to the pound in the late 1990s when my kids were young.

She was always a bit mean, a mix between a terrier and some sort of schnauzer. She'd throw all 50 pounds of her body weight at the door whenever someone came up, and if a stranger reached out a hand, she'd bite.

No matter how many times I told people, "She's not friendly," there was always some dog lover bound and determined to prove that they could pet Scout without incident. They were usually wrong.

Scout was also the best companion in the world for my youngest child, who was barely one year old when Scout joined the family. They literally grew up together. We'd often find my youngest curled up in Scout's bed, with her favorite blanket thrown over both of them.

Once we found our daughter reading a bed time story to the dog. I asked what it was about, to which she replied, "Cats, of course!" I should have known.

The Demographics of Student Debt

Our youngest is now in high school. The oldest is in college and the middle one is months away from going to college. These are the people for whom we bought the dog, so having Scout pass away with the kids nearing the time to leave home seemed perfect.

Interestingly, it was also predictable, and it's something that we at Dent Research have been predicting for decades.

Now, I had no way to know that Scout would pass away in 2011. What I DID know was that consumer demand for veterinarian services peaks at age 46, which makes perfect sense. We get married around 26, have kids around 28-30, and by the time the kids are three or four years old they're pestering us parents for cats and dogs.

Twelve to 14 years later those animals are reaching the end of their natural mortality. At this point, we as parents are in our mid to late 40s, the kids are busy with school, friends, and sports, and so often we don't replace the pet... which leads to a decline in vet visits.

Knowing this would have helped Haley Schafer immensely. She's the young lady (30 years old) who was profiled in the *New York Times* a few weeks ago.

As a newly minted veterinarian she has hit a job market that is overrun with vets. According to the article, vet visits peaked in 2006-2007. Given that the peak number of births in the U.S. was 1961, from our calculation (adding 1961 to 46, the peak age for vet visits), the peak year should have been 2007.

This means Haley was pursuing the education needed for her dream career just as the market was turning south. And Haley wasn't alone. Apparently class size at vet school has been increasing dramatically, by as much as 20% in a year.

So there are more vets coming out of school and there's a declining need for the service. Well, we know what that means. Fewer jobs and lower pay. Turns out this is exactly the case.

Over the last decade the starting salary for vets has fallen by around 13% when adjusted for inflation, down to $45,575. While this number isn't a terrible starting income, it could make it difficult to pay back student loan debt.

And Haley is carrying over $300,000 in student loans. Yep, that's right... almost one-third of a million dollars in student loans to become a veterinarian. While her debt load is extreme, the experience of a high price tag for the education is not.

The Association of American Veterinary Medicine Colleges estimates that out-of-state tuition, fees and living expenses run the average student $63,000 per year... and that costs have increased 35% over the last decade. Keep in mind, this is while starting incomes have fallen.

That's why Haley needed us. More specifically, why Haley's parents should have read our work and attended our conferences.

Kids going to college are akin to entrepreneurs. They're starting out their lives in a business or industry, so they need to take the time to estimate how the economy and world are going to change during their careers. Haley's parents could have done this on her behalf.

This is one of the areas where our demographic and consumer spending research shines. Imagine being able to estimate future demand for cars, clothes, camping equipment… almost anything! Using such information a family can make much better choices about what avenues young people pursue and how their education dollars are spent.

This might not have changed Haley's path, but at least she could feel confident that she made her decisions while knowing all the facts.

P.S. Just to prove that God has a sense of humor, after our dog passed away my wife was adamant that we would *not* get another one. The job of cleaning up after Scout and generally caring for her had fallen to her because the kids were so involved in other things. This lasted six months. We now have an 11-month old puppy that looks amazingly like our old dog… just a lot less mean.

CHAPTER 5:
CONSUMER SPENDING

The sign announcing 50% off in the window of the store doesn't matter if you're not looking at the store. I'm just not sure that politicians and government bureaucrats get this.

Consumers spend on *their* schedule, not on some predetermined schedule set by, and manipulated by, the Fed or anyone else. And yet, this is how we get idiotic policy like exceptionally low interest rates. "Set the rates, and they will come," the Fed tells us. Clearly, this is dead wrong.

The problem is that the members of the Fed and others don't account for two things: changing psychology and savings. If we're feeling more conservative, we save more. If we're preparing for a different time in our lives, like retirement, we save more. Other than offering a lifetime annuity with no strings attached, there isn't much the government can do to change this.

This matters because personal consumption is such a large part of economic activity. As a group, consumers are the 800-lb gorilla. By watching consumer spending, we get incredible insight into how people view the current economy, and therefore where things are headed next.

—Rodney Johnson

CONSUMER SPENDING

Lack of Consumer Spending is Slowing the Economy

August, 2012

Sometimes your age rears up and slaps you in the face…

A recent American Express poll of $450K+ earners revealed that this group is cautious about the U.S. economy. Sixty percent of those in the group believe we're in a recession that will last at least a year. Their savings rates are up from an average of 12% to 34%, with more going into cash or savings accounts and less into stocks.

Reports suggest that upscale consumers are moving from top-of-the-line cars to the next model down.

Welcome to the next phase of the consumer spending slowdown. This phase reaches all the way up the economic food chain. Considering that this group is responsible for 50% of personal consumption, expect the knock-on effects to be super-sized.

And it's happening right on schedule…

Back in the late 1980s, we forecast a tremendous economic boom in the U.S — and around the world —with the notable exception of Japan. We saw a long bust ahead for Japan.

The U.S. boom was supposed to usher in a period of unparalleled prosperity that would last until 2008. After that, we'd lose our economic footing… and struggle to regain it for a decade.

Our main premise was that the baby boomers would fuel a consumption bubble as they raised their children. That bubble would burst as the children left home and the boomers turned their attention to paying down debts and saving for retirement.

Our research showed that consumption peaks around age 48. Most boomers would be 48 years old in 2008-2009.

As the saying goes: "We nailed that one!"

In terms of major forecasts, this one was on the money. But as with most estimates of change in complex systems, there's more to it than meets the eye.

Five Years Later...

Digging further into consumer spending patterns, we're able to parse out more finely tuned forecasts about different groups of consumers. As it turns out, those with more money, who are also responsible for more spending, peak a little bit later.

High earners tend to be those with more education. Attending college takes up time so college graduates tend to marry a little later. They start a family later and so the kids don't leave until mom and dad are in their early- to mid-50s. The result?

Consumers with more education, earnings, and wealth tend to peak in their spending in their early 50s, five years later than the Average Joe.

Given that the overall peak in boomer spending was around 2008, we should see the next phase of this slowdown affect high earners in 2013 and 2014. As they notch down their spending, it will cause a major drag on the U.S. economy. It might not be that Williams & Sonoma shoppers are suddenly rushing into Wal-Mart, but a general reduction in spending by this group will be painful, no doubt.

Seeing big risks over the next two years, based on very predictable spending patterns, might sound like a negative... but it's not. It's a chance to take a critical view of where we are today.

We have a fiscal cliff of tax hikes and spending cuts looming... nothing but partisan voices screaming at each other over thorny issues like Medicare and Social Security... and now a deeper slowdown in consumption by the upper crust.

Since the equity markets in the U.S. are near four-year highs, it's a great time to lock in gains and take a few positions that will benefit when markets roll over.

And doubt not: they will roll over.

Want is a Powerful Thing

October, 2012

I have three kids and I found out early on that discipline must take various forms.

Each kid is different. There are "time outs" and "alone time" and taking away extravagances like TV time, video games, etc. Each of these will work to a varying degree on different children… with one big exception, my son.

For whatever reason, his personality leads him to a simple life with few wants. That made him hard to discipline. What do you take away, or for that matter give to, a child with few wants?

Time out? Alone time? Those just meant that I quit bothering him.

No extravagances? Banished to his room? "Perfect. No noise and I get to read all I want," was his response.

It was frustrating because it took a lot of patience to find what would get him to change his behavior when he got out of line… which leads me to the economy and a bunch of people who are currently "out of line" and seemingly not motivated by "want."

What's a government to do?

Baby boomers came through life with clear goals: more indulgence in the late '60s and '70s (drugs, sex and rock 'n roll)… more money in the '80s and '90s (Yuppies, BMWs and the movie *Wall Street*)… and then more of, well, everything in the late '90s and 2000s (McMansions and Hummers).

This made the boomers easier to sway. The government could extend or take away the path to the things they wanted through regulation, fiscal policy, and even monetary policy.

And it worked.

If things slowed down, the government just lowered interest rates and lending standards and the economy would turn back up on a dime as consumers took on more debt to spend on stuff.

Now, things are different. At this point the boomers are a lot like my son. As they age and move to a new stage of life, they increasingly recognize a world where "less is more," and it's giving the government fits.

Nothing the government tries is having the desired effect anymore.

With the largest number of boomers born in 1961, all of those babies are now solidly past their peak spending age of 50 and are into their peak saving years.

No longer do 22" rims on their neighbor's new Escalade sway boomers. Square footage in a home is now something that is air conditioned but not used as the children move away.

The world has changed for this group. The next target on their radar is retirement, which requires a lot bigger nest egg than they have today. So the path is to spend less, save more and pay down debt. While there is nothing magical about this change, we can't overstate its effect. When the largest generation in the economy chooses the path of less spending, it leaves the government with a set of useless tools.

The proof of this is everywhere.

Nothing Left But Blunt Instruments

The Fed has taken extraordinary measures in the last four years, all aimed at enticing consumers to spend more than they otherwise would. This has included lower interest rates for those that borrow and even negative (after inflation) interest rates for savers.

Not to be outdone, the Federal Government gave us programs like Cash for Clunkers.

Did these programs work? Sure, to a small degree, but they didn't rejuvenate the economy in a meaningful way. They didn't lead consumers, particularly baby boomers, to rekindle the buying spirit.

The die is cast. boomers won't be rejoining the "spend with abandon" class again. It's a clear case where demographics — as noted by the boomer generation passing to their next stage of life — trumps policy.

This change in particular has been one of our main forecasts for many years. Back in the early 1990s, using our Spending Wave, we estimated that baby boomers would march higher in their consumption until the late 2000s and then pull in their horns. This would leave the U.S. exposed to a massive downturn.

While the bad news is that this sort of large economic shift happens, the good news is that, with the right tools, you can see it coming decades ahead of time. And there is a bright spot...

Just as our research told us to use caution in 2008 and the years following, there are positive signs for the years after this economic season is over. Using our demographic wave and consumer spending research, we're forecasting a resurgence in the U.S. economy based on the younger generation.

Of course, it won't happen because of government policy. It will happen in spite of it.

Consumer Spending is Down, Even With Lower Interest Rates

September, 2012

For years there have been conspiracy theories about NASA. Did it really send men to the moon? Is the money for NASA funneled to some black ops group that does hush-hush things around the world?

Well, you don't have to wonder anymore. I've figured out the truth about NASA. The space agency is really just a division of the Federal Reserve.

After talking up the economy, forcing interest rates through zero into true negative numbers, and printing dollars with abandon, the Fed has finally thrown its Hail Mary pass. It bankrolled the Mars Rover in a last ditch attempt to find a new export market for the U.S... and it's desperately hoping that Martians want iPads and will pay for them in precious metals.

OK... maybe that's not true... but it might as well be.

Of course, this desperate need to find worry-free consumers willing to spend with abandon is not limited to the U.S.

China is slowing down. Its manufacturing index is flashing contraction.

The euro zone is in recession.

Japanese exports are off, exposing the worst trade deficit of recent times. And here at home the trajectory is lower.

As exports slow down there's only one way to keep growth on track: domestic consumption. But what if those pesky consumers don't do their job? What if they try to save instead of spend? Well, that's when central banks give them a nudge.

This is where things stand today. The largest markets in the world are slowing down in concert. Each nation or economic zone is trying desperately to ramp up greater exports to spur growth, but of course their normal export clients are slowing as well. So each market has its central bank taking action to spur local consumption. They're peddling lower interest rates, lower reserve rates, easier credit, expansion of money supply, you name it. And it's not working.

This is where we get yet another failed policy initiative. This is where consumers and conservative investors get to find out how they'll be punished for the umpteenth time for wanting to save for their future.

This is where it pays to be smart.

In the face of this situation we have to remain diligent, we have to stay focused on what is really going on in the world.

This global economic stall calls for building a personal war chest, creating streams of income and being ready to play markets to the downside.

This is NOT the time to buy the hype of "good times to come." Unless, of course, you're certain Martians are patiently biding their time before they claim a seat in the G20.

What Kids DON'T Want for Christmas

December, 2013

My son went to college armed with a joint bank account, shared with me. This allowed me to deposit funds easily by transferring from my account to the joint account... it also allowed me to see what he was buying. Given that most kids don't carry cash, I was able to track his spending in minute detail.

It didn't take long for him to figure it out.

By the third month he told me he was getting a job and then depositing his earnings into a separate bank account, at a different bank.

Fine!

He called a few days later, somewhat surprised that when he opened his new account at the credit union on campus they were actually going to charge him money to hold his account.

Welcome to the world of service fees, my son.

But this was just the first of many revelations he had during his first year on his own...

He began to notice that the consumer world is full of businesses that want to separate you from your money.

As he's made his way, he has become something of a miser, viewing every transaction suspiciously. I thought he was just an unusual 20-something, but it turns out he's normal... at least for his age.

A NerdWallet.com study of more than 1,000 shoppers over 18-year's old showed interesting results. The company asked about general buying habits and plans for this holiday season in particular.

It found that people under 30 are the least likely to go into debt to buy holiday gifts. As one respondent noted, if the recipients really care about you, they wouldn't want you going into debt just to buy them stuff.

That's a far cry from the way those in the 60+ category responded. This group is more likely than the youngsters to go into debt. They're also the most likely to shop by convenience, foregoing sales, discounts, and bargains.

So the aging boomers are somewhat insensitive to price, while the kids are counting nickels.

Depressingly, it makes sense. The boomers have the cash, while the kids are still looking for jobs.

As I wrote to you before, median income has been stuck in neutral for years. In fact, adjusted for inflation, median income has been dropping for half a decade. But if we sort the data by age, a different picture emerges.

While the 15- to 24-year-old group has lost 11.6% of its income since the early 1970s and 17.6% of its income since its peak, the 55- to 65-year-old group has gained 16.7% since the 1970s and only lost 7.7% of its income since the top. The older group also has lower unemployment.

Looked at in this way, it makes perfect sense that their views of spending are so different. People with steady jobs and good income aren't so worried about the future.

The problem with this is obvious.

If the young people in our economy are rightfully concerned about their financial situation and what lies ahead, what will compel them to make the life choices — like marriage and kids — that tend to drive our economy?

Cashing in on Nerds, Geeks, and Grandpas

November, 2013

We spend a lot of time pointing out the flaws in our economy, but we recognize that a lot of money continues to be made and spent. There's no question that cash is flowing, it's just not an even stream to all — or even most — participants.

While younger households, in general, are failing to keep up with inflation, those headed by older Americans are surging ahead.

At the same time, when we divide the younger households by education and profession, we see that those focused on science, technology, engineering, and math (STEM) are at the top of the money charts.

All of this means that nerds, geeks, and grandpas are moving forward economically... and they like to spend money.

So it's no surprise that industries focused on these groups are enjoying strong sales...

Companies that make recreational vehicles (RVs) and pontoon boats have done very well and are estimating higher earnings in the quarters ahead, and they're not alone.

Luxury car manufacturers and high-end appliance makers are also in on the act.

Does it mean the recession or long slog of the economy is over?

No. Not by a long shot.

It simply means that we're not dead.

Just because our overall economy is in the doldrums doesn't mean there won't be pockets of growth.

Frankly, people like to have fun. They like to have nice things.

If the world looks like it is coming to an end (remember February 2009?), then it makes sense that most people would hold off on every purchase beyond necessities. But it's been almost five long years since then. People want a break, and they don't want to feel bad about it. So, those who can afford it are stepping out and stepping up. They're buying.

As mentioned above, this doesn't mean that the all-clear bell is ringing for the economy. It simply means that those with income are pursuing their own wish lists.

As business owners and investors, our goals should include getting in front of these groups so we can benefit along the way.

RVs are an easy example because they're so clearly geared toward empty nesters and retirees. As long as fuel remains at tolerable (notice I didn't say reasonable) levels, then RV sales and related businesses like storage, cleaning, and repair should also stay busy. Along those same lines, companies like Winnebago should continue to benefit from the trend.

Nerds and geeks might be a bit harder to pin down, but the point remains the same. The market here is probably luxury cars and premium items, like $800 strollers, that appeal to young families. The vanity brands that are part of bringing up baby should also do well with this group.

So the next time you get frustrated with fiscal or monetary policy, or happen to see a statistic on how many people are working part time, just remember that there are groups who are doing quite well... then go out and find a way to profit from them!

It'll make you feel better, and then you can spend more as well.

A Conversation to Have With the Kids

December, 2013

Years ago an older couple lived next door to us. Thankfully, they delighted in our children. That made the occasional apology for sports equipment on the lawn and cars parked across their driveway a little easier. We enjoyed their company as well and were almost always happy to hear from them. Almost.

The exception was not a call from them personally, but instead a call from a sales representative for Cutco Knife company. He said our neighbors had referred him to us.

The rep was a college kid working on a scholarship and simply wanted to demonstrate the company's products to hone his craft.

Right.

My wife agreed to an appointment and then told me about it later.

Did we need knives? Not really. New ones are sharper, but we were muddling through our daily eating just fine. Before he arrived I suggested we set a spending limit of $200. My wife scoffed. Knives aren't that expensive.

Right.

The young man came to the door and proceeded to go through his show. He used a knife to cut a penny and then cut a tomato. Cool. He talked the whole time about earning his way through college. He talked about warranties and lifetime sharpening for free. He explained that the company made the K-Bar knife for our military. Very cool… and very convincing. We found ourselves wanting knives.

Then he showed us all the different knives available — steak, filet, paring, butcher, etc. Finally — finally! — he showed the master set that could be had for a low, low price of $1,200. I think my wife fainted, or at least felt a little woozy.

Summing up our fortitude, we dutifully looked through the list of what he was offering and compared it against our predetermined list of knives in our kitchen that might need replacing. All the while we kept our spending limit in mind. The overlap was small.

What struck me about the entire engagement was the force of the persuasion and the completeness of the package. The young man called us due to a referral from our dear (darn them!) neighbors. He spoke about scholarship and working. He demonstrated the strength of the knives and their resilience, and then he touched on patriotism by connecting the company to the military.

At the conclusion he opened a notebook to a page with our names on the top and then turned the book toward us. The page had ten lines on it under the headings "Name," "Address," and "Phone Number."

The young man proceeded to tell us that his success in earning his scholarship depended on his ability to see more people and that the company didn't market. Instead, it relied on the references provided by the very clients that become part of the Cutco family, or the people who had graciously agreed to a demonstration.

So, if we would be so kind as to provide the names and contact information for ten of our friends and family in the area, he could continue on his quest for higher education and life fulfillment! The young man handed me a pen.

This was a fabulous sales pitch. It had everything. Every detail was covered, and at the end we, as clients, were being given a pen and a blank piece of paper that screamed out for action.

How do you decline to provide even one name? Who is so lame or so callous as to turn away bright young lads or ladies simply looking to further their education?

Apparently, I am.

I closed the book and turned it back around. I handed him his pen and told him simply that we did not know a single other person who could use such incredible cutlery. It was as if I dared him to question me.

He was very, very quiet. Then he lost.

There's a saying in sales that he who speaks first after the gauntlet is thrown down loses. I don't know if it's true, but this young man spoke first. He thanked us and left. But he didn't leave empty handed. The adventure cost us roughly $230, for which we received four knives. Given the situation, I saw this as a victory.

I told my wife that the company had spent 60 years perfecting a sales pitch. We had spent 90 minutes listening to it. Every phrase was crafted, every reference rehearsed. This is the stuff that works. The proof is in the pudding, just look around one day at the never-ending sales pitch intruding from all sides. Billboards, radio, TV, magazines, storefronts, websites, etc.

The notion of advertising to inform is dead. It's to sell, and then to sell more. Buy because your friend said it was good. Buy because you want to support me. Buy because it's patriotic. Buy to be sexy. Whatever you do, buy.

Given the number of ads we're exposed to every day, it's amazing that any of us have any savings at all!

And yet, that is exactly what we need.

A common refrain is that we need to teach our children skills that allow them to be productive citizens. I get that, and I agree. But there's more.

We need to teach them what to do with their economic power once they have it. Buying in response to advertising — or a very persuasive sales pitch — isn't necessarily bad. The product or service can be the exact thing that a person needs or desires. The problem arises when we buy simply *because* of the ad or sales pitch, filling our days and our homes with redundant or useless things.

Teaching our kids how to budget, how to deal with finances, and how to resist the daily barrage of sales-oriented information they receive can help them achieve economic success well beyond our own.

By recognizing the difference between what others want to sell and what they want to purchase, our children can become discriminating consumers. This can help us turn away, just a little bit, from a culture of commerce and hopefully rebuild the bulwark of the middle class — savings.

I've had this conversation with my own children many a night at the dinner table. Often, with a Cutco knife close at hand.

You Know You're a Redneck When...

July, 2013

The other day my wife and I went to a local, open air food market that has part of its operation in an old building. There were the typical go-green organic foodies and soap sellers, along with people who were "upcycling" (taking discarded items and making useable stuff) by creating jewelry out of beer bottle caps.

We were there for the vegetable sellers, the local dairy producers who bring in farm fresh eggs, and the local butcher. I have to admit that I am usually skeptical of such places, but there is no question that the food does taste better. I use this point to give me a reason for being there in the first place.

It always strikes me as odd that we spent over 100 years perfecting ways to grow, harvest, store, and transport food so that it would be right there at the grocery store, available and inexpensive, and yet people with disposable income want to go backwards.

We (and yes, I'm in the group, whether I like it or not) gladly pay two or three times more for food if it has been grown by some recluse in his yard down the street versus being grown on some 10,000 acre farm by Archer Daniels Midland (ADM) in the middle of the country.

But like I said... the "fresh" food does taste better, and since it's *our* disposable income, we can spend it how we choose.

Even if that choice seems silly...

In this particular open air market, inside the old building, was a "grow wall." Being not-so-informed about new growing techniques, I was not privy to this process. I was the guy staring at the wall, wondering what idiot would grow things sideways... on a wall... when there was a perfectly level field out back?

And this thing wasn't just stuck up there. It was a man-sized erector set!

For those in the dark like I was, a growing wall is a wide expanse of a wall (this one was 20 feet high and sixty feet long) on which a farmer hangs plants to grow out from the wall.

On the one I saw, there were three columns of 3' x 2' boxes that were further divided into nine squares. These boxes and dividers were made out of stainless steel, and were packed full of dirt, with plants sticking outward from them. There were tomatoes, eggplant, spices, lettuce, and all sorts of other things. A drip irrigation system fed into each large box, which both hydrated the plants and kept the soil moist enough to stop the dirt from crumbling out.

About two feet away from the wall hung huge 2' x 5' light fixtures, with the lights pointing at the wall. They were connected to a long piece of steel, hanging down like a Calder Mobile. The lights slowly moved left and then right in front of the grow wall.

Like I said, this was an amazing set up.

The "farmer" tending to this crop was eager to explain it to us. I asked a lot of questions, which he enthusiastically answered. I hid my amazement that this could in any way be an efficient or cost effective endeavor… right up until the end, when he told me who buys the vegetables.

They deliver the trays — meaning the plants are still in the dirt — to high-end restaurants, who then put them on display and harvest the food for their menu.

Really?!

Farmer Dave continued explaining…

His goal is to open a "pick your own" grow wall, where (gullible) consumers can come in and harvest right off the wall. "Wouldn't that be cool?" he asked. Oh my.

I know I must be showing my heritage because I found all of this ridiculous. I couldn't escape the simple conclusion that we, as a society, are incredibly rich… to the point that we would not only choose to go backward in food production, but would spend money at such a rate as to support a process whereby food is grown vertically on a wall!

As we left the place I expressed some of this to my wife, who reminded me that farming is not only a good thing to understand, but it also provides great ingredients for meals while helping local growers. And, as I mentioned above, there is no question that fresh food… even grown on a wall… tastes better than what you'd find from the local grocery chain, where the food is often picked more than sixty days, some 1,000 miles away, before your hands touch it.

Still, I can't help but think how bizarre this situation has become.

With terms like locavore (a person who only eats what can be grown or raised in the immediate area) entering our daily lexicon, there has been an incredible move to focus on food production, even though we have more than enough.

At a time when more than half of Americans have little or no retirement savings, when 35% of Social Security recipients count on that measly check for over 90% of their income, why are we not focused on personal sustainability instead of local food?

Why are parents teaching their kids about how to grow tomatoes instead of, or at least in addition to, how to grow a savings account for college, marriage, a home, and retirement? It all seems sort of backwards.

The only thing I know for sure is that somewhere a bunch of farmers are laughing really loudly about all those city folk picking vegetables grown under lights hanging on walls. Unfortunately none of us will be laughing in 20 to 30 years when all those well-fed people are looking for financial support in their old age.

STUDENT LOANS

Worst Business Idea of the Decade

August, 2013

Imagine you get a call from an uncle pitching an investment idea. He wants you to join him in bankrolling a pool of start-up ventures with a very high payoff potential. In the past, businesses like those in the pool have earned around 500% over their lifetimes. Of course, there have been some failures.

It sounds pretty good, so you ask some questions.

Do the entrepreneurs have experience in their businesses? No.

Is there a high rate of success in the pool? No, in fact about one-third fails.

As an investor, do you get control over the businesses? No.

Do you have a clear equity position? No, actually, you're a lender and the loans are unsecured.

Do you earn above market returns? No, in fact you lend at some of the lowest rates in the country, so the 500% return goes to the business owners, not the investors.

Do the borrowers have a great repayment record? Nope, instead they default at a much higher rate than most other types of loans.

Hmmm.

At this point, you'd think your uncle was crazy. Who in their right mind would make an unsecured loan to an inexperienced business person where the rate of failure is high, the rate of default is high, and the rate of return for the loan itself is extraordinarily low?

Unfortunately, more people than you'd think... because this story isn't very hypothetical. It's actually how federal student loans work, and Uncle Sam is coercing us into joining the program.

The Consumer Finance Protection Board (CFPB) recently released statistics on how the Federal Student Loan program is working out...

Given the market is now over $1 trillion and still growing rapidly, understanding the repayment history of the program can be instructive and important for those of us footing the bill.

The findings are not encouraging.

About $315 billion of all student loans are held by people still in school or in some other way deferred, meaning the repayment process hasn't begun.

Of the $685 billion remaining, $180 billion are in forbearance or default. That's a rate of 26% of the total value of loans outstanding that are currently in the repayment period. This is close to the same percentage of borrowers behind on their loans, at 22%.

Over the last several years, the U.S. has experienced an explosion in college applications and attendance. It seems everyone got the message that education is required for success later in life. This is why so many student-loan borrowers have yet to enter the repayment phase... but they will.

In the years ahead, millions of new graduates — who are also new student-loan borrowers — will hit the streets looking for jobs. Right now our economy is creating around 150,000 jobs per month, most of which are part-time and being filled by workers aged 55 to 64.

To say that recent graduates are struggling to find financially rewarding careers would be a gross understatement. That means down the road we can expect the student-loan default rate to at least remain the same, if not get worse. But there's a caveat...

As lenders, you and I gave borrowers a way to pay back less than they owe.

The federal government set up income-based repayment plans, where borrowers can contract to pay back a percentage of their income, no matter how small the absolute amount is, for a set number of years. When the time frame has passed, the remaining student loans are forgiven.

To give this program even more horsepower, the government made it so those in public-service jobs can be finished with their loans over a shorter time frame... which means they pay back even less.

As an investor, this is akin to allowing your borrowers to make variable payments based on their profit, where the payments will always be less than you would have received under the original terms of the notes, and then forgiving any loan balances remaining after 20 years.

This of course makes no business sense, and it makes no sense for our government. But that's okay. We'll do it anyway. Maybe we can make up any losses by increasing our lending volume.

This situation is going to boil over in the years ahead.

We're creating a growing class of educated young people who are willfully choosing to saddle themselves with unaffordable debt because they're too young to understand the reality of economics… and because they've been brainwashed all their lives to believe this is the path to a better life.

As they reach their late 20s and early 30s without being able to afford to grow their personal lives through getting married, having kids, or simply buying the trappings of the middle class, they'll get frustrated and demand relief. The only way they'll find that relief is if government saddles American taxpayers with yet another burden.

If you pay taxes… watch out.

Gaming the Student Loan System

October, 2013

Some people are really proud of their college. They wear jerseys on game days, put stickers on their cars, even get tattoos.

I don't go so far as all that.

My proclamation of support is wearing an old baseball cap when I do yard work or sail. It's just like my last battered baseball cap, which now resides somewhere at the bottom of Tampa Bay, after being knocked off in a storm.

Still, once in a while someone will notice my hat and ask if I graduated from Georgetown University (GU), and I quickly respond: "Yes!" After all, everyone likes to belong to well-regarded institutions. We point to our school's reputation for sports, academics, or whatever it is that makes the place standout.

Now my alma mater, or at least its law school, has developed a new way to stand out...

It has created an interesting way to game the student loan system.

Stirring up a witch's brew, Georgetown Law concocted a scheme that merges three programs to create a blockbuster offering for students — free law school.

The first program is the graduate student-loan system that allows students to borrow every cent they need for tuition, fees, books, and living expenses. Everything! The U.S. government originates these student loans, as it does all student loans these days.

The second program is Income-Based Repayment for student loans. Under this plan a graduate who gets a government job (or almost any non-profit job) can opt to pay back a set percentage of his modest salary for 10 years. After that the government forgives what remains of his student loan.

The third program is how the university sets tuition, which is any way it wants.

This blockbuster combination requires students to borrow every nickel needed for school, to get a public service jobs after graduation and to apply for the 10-year Income-Based Repayment plan. At that point, GU Law commits to making all the student loan payments required. How would the school get the money needed to make the payments? By setting tuition a little higher on the front end, of course!

This program is a thing of beauty that creates winners all around... well, almost all around. There is one group that gets the short end of the stick.

Taxpayers.

Some altruistic billionaire doesn't fund the Income-Based Repayment program. This brain child is an offering of our U.S. government, and presumably was meant to encourage people to join public service.

No matter what the motivation, the end result is obvious: non-repayment of millions, if not billions, of dollars in student loans, with taxpayers picking up the bill.

And it gets better.

Many people have labeled Georgetown Law's program as an abuse of the system, one that allows students to foist payment onto someone else. This is true, but it misses one of the most elegant parts of the scheme.

In the world of private industry — be it banking, health care, manufacturing or most anything else — one of the most frustrating elements is compliance with ever-changing government regulations.

To stay on the right side of the law, companies hire either in-house compliance specialists or consulting firms filled with bright young people who are knowledgeable about such things.

The absolute best person to have on your side when you're trying to navigate regulation is a person who recently worked within the government, either setting or enforcing said regulation. Such people have intimate working knowledge of how the rules are enforced, what areas of the law are most important, and they even have personal relationships with staff members within the enforcement agencies.

There's a price that companies pay for such people, and it's high. It comes in the form of salaries and bonuses. People with firsthand knowledge of regulations are in high demand.

So a common career path for a bright, young lawyer is to work within a government agency for, say, 10 years, to gain invaluable knowledge and relationships, and then "flip" to the private sector to boost his pay by several hundred percent.

This is where the Georgetown Law program shines. It shows students how to get a free education, which even the school doesn't pay for, and how to use their 10 years of government servitude to set themselves up for a lifetime of high earnings that kick in right after their student loans are forgiven.

Brilliant!

Given that Georgetown Law costs about $75,000 per year (including tuition, living expenses, etc.), the estimated cost of this program to taxpayers is $158,000 in forgiven debt per student.

And now other schools are jumping on the band wagon. Both Berkeley and Duke are pitching their own, similar programs.

While I recognize that this program is innovative and seeks to use available resources to their full advantage, I find it difficult to square this with any sense of fair play and the "spirit" of the programs involved instead of the actual letter of the law.

I think now when people ask if I attended Georgetown I'll still answer yes, but I'll quickly point out that it was for undergraduate study.

CHAPTER 6:
Health Care

Health care is a lightning rod. Not only does it draw incredible energy from the atmosphere that creates the flash of light in the sky, it also handles a groundswell of energy that comes up from the earth. We are in the throes of dealing with the massive costs — mandated insurance, surtax on medical devices, surtax on capital gains, etc. — of the Affordable Care Act at the same time that the new law has provided newfound access to the health care system for millions of Americans.

The issue is not solved by any stretch of the imagination, because all we've done is increase access, not limit cost. As we do this, there will be a lot of gnashing of teeth and tearing of cloth by special interest groups who stand to lose hundreds of billions of dollars in revenue. It can't come a minute too soon.

—Rodney Johnson

HEALTH CARE

Where Are All the Doctors?

April, 2012

Need a doctor?

Then get your passport ready.

Because, the way things are shaping up in our health care system, you'll be lucky to find a doctor who can help you.

As it turns out, there aren't nearly enough doctors and nurses in the U.S. to provide the care we need. The Association of Medical Colleges reported last year that, by 2020, the U.S. health care system will have a shortage of 90,000 doctors. According to Dr. Peter Buerhaus, we're also facing a shortage of 260,000 nurses.

And with the baby boomers entering their golden years, the pressure on the health care system is only going to get worse. There's nothing magic about this forecast. Older people need more care, which requires more care providers...

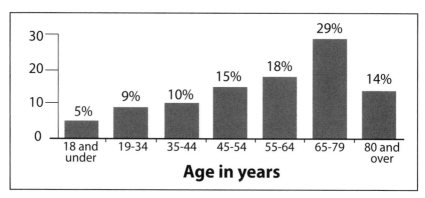

And our economy is not generating enough new health care professionals to meet the upcoming demand.

It's All About Money

Ultimately, this problem comes down to a matter of money: there's simply not enough of it to increase enrollments in medical and nursing schools across the country.

For example, Wayne State University in Michigan has a renowned nursing program. It receives over two thousand applicants a year and admits around 350. That's all it has space for because medical programs have strict limitations on the student/teacher ratios they must maintain to keep accreditation.

While this might seem like a bureaucratic limitation, the reason it's in place is to ensure the learning opportunity for each candidate in the hands-on parts of the programs.

So, the only way for schools to maintain these ratios AND increase admissions is to add more teaching staff. But that costs money. And most publicly funded universities are in cost-cutting mode right now. Don't expect anything to change in a hurry.

The shortage is medical professionals will only get worse.

The question then is, how do you get the medical care you or your parents might need in the next few years?

The answer is: turn to medical tourism.

Not only will you find highly skilled medical practitioners and specialists in emerging countries like India, but you'll often find doctors considered the best in their fields... and you'll likely pay much less for your treatment.

For example, you'd only pay $1,900 for a heart operation in India. The same operation in the U.S. would cost you around $60,000.

Knee replacement surgery in India, Costa Rica or Mexico costs between $6,000 and $12,500. In the U.S., you're looking at $40,000.

A kidney transplant in India starts at $17,000. Back in 2005, the average cost to transplant one kidney in the U.S., ranged from $210,000 to over $800,000.

Cataract surgery, back surgery, lung cancer surgery. You name it and you'll more easily find top-notch doctors in emerging markets AND pay only a fraction of the price.

This makes emerging markets, like India, the place to watch for massive investment gains in the years to come (not yet, mind you). They're positioning themselves to take advantage of demographic shifts in the developed nations and they have their own demographic wave flooding their economies.

There's a big boom ahead.

Pharmaceutical Companies are Happy — Old People are Buying Drugs

September, 2012

Okay, I'm not talking about illicit drugs. There are not many arrest reports for 60-somethings trolling the streets for crack cocaine, although the baby boomers are making marijuana arrests a more common occurrence.

Instead, I'm referring to the incredible increase in pharmaceutical use that happens as people age past 55, particularly in the 65- to 75-year old range.

This trend is well known. It's been discussed in a million publications. You've no doubt heard, many times, how big drug companies are set to make a killing (no pun intended) in the years ahead.

So why do we care?

We care because it's not about the drugs. It's not about the pharmaceutical companies ...

This is about consumers doing things en masse, in very predictable ways... and how this allows us to forecast what they will do next. This demand curve illustrates my point beautifully...

What you see here is one of thousands of demand curves we've created and use to stay ahead of the curve in hundreds of different industries.

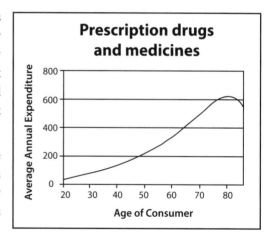

Armed with this knowledge, the sky is the limit when it comes to running a business, buying or selling real estate, choosing a career and, of course, investing.

The key is: understand what drives people to buy.

Governments want you, as a consumer, to steadily increase your spending as you get older. They want you to hit the familiar milestones like purchasing a car and buying a house.

The government wants you to use credit to keep up your spending, even when your income suffers. By doing this, you help the economy remain on a steady path higher.

If you falter, you screw up the system. That's when the government tries to persuade you to fall back into line. It uses lower interest rates, tax incentives, reduced income on savings — anything it can conceive of to get you to move your money (be it saved or borrowed) into the economic grindstone.

But today we are at a point where people are simply not complying. They don't want more "stuff." In fact, they want less of something — debt.

The reality is that the largest group in our economy, the boomers, has turned the economic corner. They've moved from their highest point of spending to their peak saving years. As such, they're no longer adding to the growth of the economy.

The government keeps trying to prod them along, but to no avail!

These consumers are not responding because it doesn't fit what they need in their personal lives. It doesn't matter what the government wants for the economy as a whole.

We know this and have been talking to audiences and readers about it, for more than two decades, through our publications, our books, our media appearances and at our conferences!

We saw these changes happening years before they occurred.

The good news is that things are constantly changing! So we use our research to pinpoint predictable consumer spending and then combine it with population trends to see what different groups will do for many years to come.

We know when beach real estate will boom again.

We have a bead on the next trend in employment.

We certainly have a forecast for what types of investments people should hold.

All of this comes out of our research on how people spend combined with the size of different groups in our economy. It's like having a trail map in a forest. There's lot going on, but there's definitely a clear path forward!

And it all starts with seeing *how* and *when* people buy things like drugs and potato chips and motorcycles.

Health Care Costs Soaring by Many Times Inflation Rate

September, 2012

The Kaiser Foundation tracks health care spending at more than 2,000 large and small employers each year. It found that, over the past year, the cost of health care insurance premiums increased by "only" 4%.

Those touting new health care regulation see this as a major victory. It shows that tough measures can work.

Hmmm.

Given that a 4% increase means cost shot higher by 235% the rate of inflation… and that in a short time it will be illegal NOT to buy health care insurance… AND the current increase is on top of a 9% increase from 2010-2011, does it really feel like a deal?

Seems like more of a scam…

Just because someone hits me less often than in the past doesn't negate the fact that they're hitting me.

And while we're on the subject of a rising cost that is shoved down our throats, let's not lose sight of the other side of this coin — how we all pay for it?

In the world of inflation, we're supposed to see our costs rise (we definitely have that), the value of our assets move higher (ugh, not so much), and the size of our paychecks and interest checks increase (actually moving lower).

To badly butcher the old Meatloaf song: "one out of three is terrible!"

If the only part of inflation that we get is higher costs, then that leads to one thing — a falling standard of living.

Welcome to America in the 2010s.

It doesn't really matter who people vote for in the November 2012 elections. The U.S. is headed down the path of less.

Many of the reasons for this trend are written in stone…

We have to pay down the debts incurred in previous years. We have to pay for entitlements promised but not funded. We have to deal with the slowdown that was telegraphed years into the future by demographics.

But there's one reason that isn't pre-destined, but chosen. That is the financial repression the Federal Reserve is forcing on seniors and all other savers. They've become more mafia than anything else.

The Fed, with Ben Bernanke as the godfather, is stealing from the till, slipping away with a percentage of all the money in the system.

Not only is this group artificially holding interest rates exceptionally low, which steals money from savers to favor borrowers, they're also printing more money as we go along, which just doubles down on the tactic of stealing from savers.

Our forecast for many years has been for deflation to take hold in the current economic climate, and that is exactly what has occurred in areas such as income and many assets such as homes.

The Fed continues to fight the trend with the only tools it has. Given that the Fed's toolbox includes all things monetary, its plan of attack has to include tinkering with money.

The basic approach is to take from those who have it and move it to those who will spend it.

It is in this environment, with incomes falling, our savings accounts earning less, and home prices in the deep freeze, that the whole notion of a 4% increase in a large, necessary cost seems outrageous.

It is NOT a bargain as the mainstream media would have you believe.

Health Exchanges: Taking Paul Ryan's Approach to Health Care

October, 2013

There's a growing wave of companies doing their level best to contain health care costs while also providing their employees and retirees with quality health care insurance.

To achieve both of these goals, the companies are kicking employees and retirees to the curb.

Well, not literally… but they are forcing them out of company-sponsored insurance programs and instructing them to find insurance on the new health exchanges. The reasons for doing this are obvious: it's easier, and in the long run it should be less expensive.

Health care benefits are a pain. It takes an incredible amount of resources for a company the size of IBM or Sears to manage these benefits.

At the same time, the future cost of health insurance is an unknown. Will rates go up by 3%, 6% or 14% next year? No one knows.

With the rollout of health exchanges, now companies can get rid of most of their administrative headaches associated with providing health benefits, and also get some sort of handle on future costs. They do this by providing employees, retirees or both with a voucher for buying health insurance instead of providing the insurance itself.

By simply providing the monetary benefit, these companies are ridding themselves of the infrastructure necessary to manage the health benefits. At the same time these companies are setting up a showdown in the future when they'll tell employees and retirees that the value of the health benefit voucher will not increase at the same rate as the cost of insurance.

This is the only way to bend the health-cost curve without actually changing the way our system provides care. In short, companies are paving the way for having employees and retirees kick in more for their own care.

An interesting point about this trend is that it sounds a lot like Rep. Paul Ryan's plan for Medicare that he floated during the last election. Under that plan, the U.S. government would solicit bids for the provision of Medicare services, and then provide to recipients a voucher equal to the second-lowest bid.

Recipients could then buy the lowest cost insurance or the second lowest cost insurance without spending any of their own money, or they could supplement the voucher with their own funds to buy a higher-priced policy.

There were wild screams and shouts from people who claimed that Ryan was taking something from them, when that was hardly the case. Would it have changed in the future, where the government switched to a voucher for only the lowest cost, or perhaps simply froze the value of the voucher while the cost of the premiums marched higher? It sure seems likely.

Unfortunately all of the recent upheavals in health care — the Affordable Care Act, moving employees and retirees to health exchanges, the proposal for Medicare — are centered on who bears the cost of insurance, when the real elephant in the room is the wildly inflated and almost indiscernible cost of care.

When a simple survey of the cost of a standard procedure like a knee replacement can vary from $11,000 to $115,000, then there's obviously a problem. None of the changes mentioned above do a single thing to fix the problem... they only change who gets the bill.

Health Care Has Jumped the Shark

February, 2013

Too many years ago the sitcom "Happy Days" was all the rage. As time went on the story went stale, so the writers kept having the characters do more outrageous things…

In one episode, the Fonz (Henry Winkler) is on vacation with the gang in California. One of the highlights of the trip is when he jumps over a shark on water skis.

Now there are all sorts of things wrong with this storyline but this isn't the place to delve into it, as much as I want to. Suffice it to say the general consensus was that when this episode appeared it was the true end of the show.

And today, whenever something has become so ridiculous it's only a shadow of its former self, it's said to have "jumped the shark."

In the world of health care, this has definitely happened…

Several weeks ago my older daughter hurt her ankle during crew practice. It had not healed in a few days so the coach wanted to have it x-rayed.

Sensing a teaching moment (as parents we have a sixth-sense for such things), I sent my daughter to a local orthopedic urgent care clinic. This was only two days after her 18th birthday.

The clinic is run by a big orthopedic center in town. I sent her with instructions to find out how much it would cost to get an x-ray and have the ankle checked out. My goal was to drive home the notion that we really can make a cost/benefit decision on health care.

We have insurance, but it's a high-deductible plan with a health savings account, so we pay the first several thousand dollars of any care. So these decisions are important.

The clinic told her she'd pay $300 for the doctor's visit and $75 for the x-ray. That seemed steep to me, but not so far out of line as to be a problem. She signed in and then called two hours later to relate her story. It went something like this…

She saw the Physician's Assistant (NOT the doctor himself) who thought she had a high ankle sprain. The x-ray confirmed this.

All of this took less than 10 minutes.

Then there was a discussion about how to immobilize the foot so it would heal faster. They offered her an inflatable walking boot for a cost of $620. She said that was a bit ridiculous and asked for alternatives. They told her an old-style short fiberglass cast was included in the $300 office visit. She took the deal.

A week later she needed to have the cast removed. When she called back, the center said: "Oh, this is not an urgent care issue. For that you'll have to become a patient, which requires a $3,000 deposit."

Again, she pointed out this was stupid.

They lowered their price to $800.

She hung up.

After searching the Internet for 20 minutes she found instructions on how to cut off the cast in the garage, which she happily did.

(Yes, I'm a proud father.)

This whole story tells me that few people "buy" health care. They consume it. To "buy" something means to pay for it. Most don't.

There is a third party involved, an insurance company, which masks the cost of every single aspect of health care. Most people would have presented their insurance card, paid the deductible, and never considered the "cost" of the different options available... which of course leads to runaway billing on the part of providers as evidenced by my daughter's experience, which isn't over yet...

After all of this, I received a bill for $408 from the clinic. It showed the visit, the x-ray, and then a separate charge of $100 for the fiberglass cast and $308 for putting it on.

My daughter confirmed that her conversation with the Physician's Assistant was clear: the cast was included in the cost of the visit. So I called the number on the bill to discuss this with a "finance consultant." I told her the story. I told her I have a receipt.

She told me the receipt just shows a payment, it doesn't mean the bill is paid.

I asked her how, if I had paid the full amount requested, was I to know that more was going to be asked of me? She told me that I would have had to ask for a detailed list of the treatments coded for my daughter. I asked how I was supposed to know that.

And she said: "I don't know."

I reiterated that the care provider had told my daughter the cost of the cast was included in the visit, and she told me that it was impossible for a Physician's Assistant to tell a patient the cost of anything because none of the providers — assistants, doctors, no one — knows what any of it costs.

As politely as I could, I asked her how a patient was supposed to determine if a treatment was worth the cost if the cost can't be presented before the treatment?

She told me: "You can't."

This is where we are.

Doctor's offices are not care provider units anymore. They're care provider units coupled with medical coding expert units. The goal is to certainly provide care, I don't doubt that, but then also to code an account for the highest possible reimbursement from the insurance company or Medicare.

Given that coding can take a myriad of forms, doctors are taken out of the equation. If I had any hope of finding out the cost of anything, I was told that my daughter would have had to check with the office manager before receiving any specific step of care.

And this is why health care is broken.

There is no financial relationship between the patient and the caregiver. If we want to have any hope of bringing the cost of care under control, we must inject the cost of treatment into the conversation at the point of care, not in a political debate 1,000 miles away.

By the way, I'm still fighting this, but as you might expect, the office manager has yet to find time to call me back.

I'm considering paying the bill.

In pennies.

Does it seem wrong to show up at their office with 40,800 pennies?

A Welcome Departure From a Depressing Norm

August, 2013

I'm getting old.

Beyond the simple fact that every day I inch forward chronologically, I also have the aches and pains of a person pushing 50. This came into stark relief last week when I tried, with one arm, to move a very heavy tent.

To get the 80-pound contraption where it needed to be, I had to lift it about a foot over my head with my arm completely extended. I got it done and then moved on to my other chores without giving it another thought.

The next morning I could hardly move my shoulder. I had excruciating pain and inflammation. I got through the required morning tasks then headed off to a walk-in clinic. By the time I got there I was beyond miserable. I walked through the door and looked straight at a huge bulletin board displaying the prices for service.

That's when the geek in me took over...

I use a Health Savings Account, which means I have insurance but it pays for nothing until I meet my deductible of about $10,000. I've never reached that level, thank goodness.

However I am a careful consumer of health care. I ask the price of everything, which as readers of this letter know, can lead to weird situations, such as health care providers not being able to tell you the cost of a service until after it has been rendered. That's why this walk-in clinic was such a nice surprise.

I knew that any health professional would want to x-ray my shoulder, and from looking at the wall I knew it would cost $127 and be performed on the property in a matter of minutes. I knew the basic visit would be $75. Immediately I began looking around and wondering about the business of the place.

I was brought to an examination room and my vital signs were taken (don't worry, I'm healthy). Within five minutes a woman came in and introduced herself as Anne, the nurse practitioner. Perfect! I'm a big fan of having most medical needs addressed by someone other than an M.D., who should spend his or her time on the most serious or difficult cases.

Anne quickly assessed my issue, surmising that I had over-exerted the shoulder and caused inflammation of the muscle and connective tissue that was impeding my movement and causing pain. She ordered an x-ray to rule out bone issues (there weren't any), and then prescribed a steroid shot to help with the swelling and a sling to stop me from damaging it further.

The entire visit lasted less than 45 minutes.

When I paid my bill of $251, I was presented with a detailed listing of the diagnosis, a course of treatment (immobilization and further non-steroidal anti-inflammatory medication), a detailed statement of what to do if the condition didn't improve, and a CD that contained the x-rays so I could take it to my primary physician.

Needless to say, I was stunned.

Here was a for-profit venture focused on the provision of immediate medical care that seemed to be clearly focused on the client. I had no idea such a business existed.

My experience with health care providers over the past decade has been frustrating at best, with fees charged after the fact, unnecessary services forced on us, and billing that showed up more than two years after services were performed.

The fact that this business was so efficient and transparent was a welcomed departure from what has become a depressing norm.

I can only hope that this sort of experience will be, or is already being, replicated around the country. It would be great to see people like me, who are fortunate enough to see a doctor very infrequently, use a system of walk-in clinics that can provide almost all of the services we'll ever need (sinus infections, strep, busted shoulder, etc.).

This is the sort of trend that can and should unfold over the next decade, leading to greater business opportunities for companies like Walgreen's and CVS Pharmacies, two of the firms that have committed to putting clinics in their retail locations.

If we finally get some efficiencies built into our provision of health care, then maybe American families wouldn't have to choose between health insurance and a new car.

Of course, the American Medical Association (AMA) won't be too happy, but that's a group we can afford to alienate.

Paying the $600 Billion Bill for Health Care is Now YOUR Problem

February, 2013

We're staring down the barrel of a loaded gun.

And the gunman's trigger finger's getting heavy.

The gun? Public pensions and retirement health care benefits.

The gunman? Money. Or lack thereof, to be more precise.

We raised the alarm, back in 2006 already, about the crisis in funding these services. Back then the problem was estimated to be a combined funding shortfall to the tune of about $500 billion. By 2008 the problem had grown to a $1 trillion shortfall. Now we're facing a $1.3 trillion black hole.

This situation continues to grow out of control because no one is making changes big enough, or fast enough, to stem the rising tide of costs.

Until now that is…

The Affordable Care Act, due to take effect in 2014, introduces a path for cities and states to move their retirees onto the rolls of public exchange health care systems… and have it paid for through federal subsidies.

In other words, we (that's me and you) get to foot the bill.

Naturally cities, states and public worker unions are giddy at the prospect because it takes a monkey off their backs. Now we get to carry it around.

In case you missed it, the Affordable Care Act requires everyone to have health insurance or else face a fine. The act also requires large employers to offer affordable care to their employees (insurance that costs less than 9.5% of income) or face a penalty.

There are some gaps in this, like for people who work at small companies or who retired before they could enroll in Medicare… or even those that don't work at all. For these people there's supposed to be access to government-sponsored insurance exchanges in each state. Each person's cost of health care will become part of their income tax calculation. At low levels of income people will receive tax credits in order to make their health care affordable.

Pensions that public entities offer tend to be backed by the full faith and credit of the entity, like the State of California or the city of Harrisburg, PA. In many states these pensions are constitutionally guaranteed and can't be reduced.

However, the same isn't true of health care benefits. In almost all cases, health care benefits for retirees are not guaranteed. These benefits can be reduced or even eliminated.

Because these costs are the fastest growing part of the underfunded problems public entities face, the idea of reducing such benefits is gaining traction. However, it would cause a political firestorm to suddenly tell millions of 55-65 year olds they don't have health care.

And this is where you and I unknowingly and involuntarily come in.

If an early retiree is too young for Medicare, they're required to seek out their own insurance from a government-sponsored exchange. Most will likely qualify for some amount of tax credit to pay for the insurance.

Voila!

Health care for millions of public pensioners now paid for by national taxpayers… thus alleviating a great burden for the original city, state or other grantor of the benefits.

Thank goodness the national taxpayers don't pay close enough attention to block such a move.

Living With the Reality of the Affordable Care Act

March, 2014

I think Jack Nicholson is crazy. I don't know him personally, but he just looks… off.

Particularly in those old films like *"Five Easy Pieces," "One Flew Over the Cuckoo's Nest,"* and *"As Good As it Gets."* Perhaps that's why his characters stick with us, long after the end credits.

Take that one line he spoke in *"A Few Good Men,"* for example.

As Colonel Jessup, Mr. Nicholson gets that crazy look in his eyes before yelling at Tom Cruise: "You can't handle the truth!"

I can't remember a single one of Mr. Cruise's lines, but like most other Americans, I can clearly see Jack Nicholson's outburst in my head.

When it comes to the Affordable Care Act (ACA), or Obamacare, it's as if we simply can't handle the truth…

People seem to be in one of two camps. They either love the idea of everyone buying insurance so much, they can't see the flaws in the plan… Or they hate the notion of the government demanding we buy insurance so much, they can't see any of the benefits.

Parts of both narratives are true. This makes the law difficult to swallow and even harder to unwind. And, of course, we have Congress to thank for the mess.

Most of the hardest-hitting parts of the ACA are not even in effect yet. For example, parts of the mandates require larger employers to provide insurance for workers at certain levels. This has driven companies and public entities, like cities and states, to limit worker hours so they stay under the threshold.

However, this requirement keeps getting pushed out or adjusted. Right now, individuals will only pay a penalty if they don't comply, after they file their 2014 taxes in 2015.

Still, the fallout has been tremendous in some areas, like the cancellation of existing policies that don't meet the benefit requirements of the law.

The Associated Press estimates that 4.7 million people were kicked off of their insurance as of December 31, 2013, which makes the current administration's claims of success a bit odd.

As of January 31, the U.S. government estimated that 3.3 million people had signed up for insurance through a health exchange. However, the insurance companies estimate that only 80% of them had paid for coverage, so the effective sign-up number was 2.7 million people.

With 4.7 million people losing coverage and only 2.7 million buying new policies, we're actually going backward.

Not included in this calculation is the fact that the U.S. government had estimated we would have six million newly insured people by the end of January. There are some mitigating factors…

No one knows how many of the 4.7 million canceled consumers joined their spouse's plan or had another path to coverage that didn't involve a health exchange. What we do know is that some people who were uninsured have now signed up for health insurance, which was the goal of the law in the first place.

Stories about people finally being able to purchase insurance aren't just tales of subsidies or the unemployed. Many hard-working, self-reliant Americans desperately wanted the simple privilege (privilege!) of paying for insurance, but had been denied because of pre-existing conditions. These people — our friends, neighbors, and family members — can now purchase health coverage and stop living in fear of medical bankruptcy.

It's a travesty that this group was unable to get health coverage at any cost in a country as rich as the U.S. before the ACA was enacted.

Unfortunately, nowhere in this story is the *real issue*: Health care is still really expensive.

Creating a system by which people not only can, but also must, buy insurance, does nothing to alleviate the cost of the care itself. To do that, we have to lift the covers and ask what really makes sense.

Does it make sense that companies can write off the cost of health-insurance premiums from their taxes, but individuals can't?

Does it make sense that we pay money to insurance companies that negotiate wildly different prices with providers than what they offer to the man on the street?

Does it make sense that two providers in the same town will offer prices on a service that can be tens of thousands of dollars apart?

Does it make sense that we've turned our doctors into box-checking uber-administrators who have to manipulate the coding of Medicare to get paid at least the cost of the service provided (which ends up sending the private billing of any service through the roof)?

The Affordable Care Act is darkly humorous because the law does nothing to make care more affordable. It just spreads the cost among more people.

Unfortunately, we can't turn back the clock. If Congress repealed the ACA, would we look at those who were only recently able to get coverage and tell them: "No, you can't have insurance anymore... Sorry!"?

Of course not.

Some form of the ACA is here to stay, even if it's called something different. The cold reality is that the hard work of reigning in health care was not accomplished, or even attempted, in the ACA. That would have required staring down special interest groups, like pharmaceutical companies, large public firms, hospitals, and the American Medical Association — something for which Congress has shown no appetite. Instead, our representatives passed a law more than 1,900 pages long and in draft form — in less than a week — before any of them had read the proposed law, much less debated it. That's not good government. That's idiocy.

We have to work on making health care not only affordable in terms of the premiums individuals pay, but also affordable to our nation as a whole. If we don't start looking at the bigger picture, health care will be the animal that ate the country.

At its current rate of growth, health care is estimated to take up more than 20% of our economy in just a few years, moving quickly toward 25%. These numbers are so big, even Jack Nicholson might be scared.

MEDICARE

Stealing From Your Kids

October, 2012

Have you ever had a stupid argument with someone you find to be, most of the time, very intelligent? Have you ever just shaken your head in disbelief that an otherwise rational person could hold that point of view?

This is the way I feel when I talk about Social Security and Medicare with people, particularly those who are current recipients.

Do they get the fact that their level of benefits, and the level promised to the millions following them in the next few years, is one of the major problems facing this country?

Do they get that their demand for a payment well beyond anything they contributed must come from the labor of their children?

Of course they do.

They must, as the facts are so obvious. But it's okay, because they are "entitled." After all, these payments are called "entitlements" for a reason, right?

The problem is that the government set up a program that was sound, then voted in changes that are terribly irresponsible. So now we are left with a stream of payments we can't afford... unless we're willing to keep stealing from our children...

Medicare is running a deficit, and will continue to do so for the foreseeable future.

Social Security is not far behind.

The two programs are "pay-as-you-go," meaning payments from current workers go mostly to pay for the benefits of current retirees. This works well as long as the pool of workers is growing faster than the pool of retirees.

Hmmm. Houston, we have a problem...

Not only have we voted in cost of living adjustments that boost payments, but we also have high numbers of baby boomers retiring, skewing the worker/retiree relationship.

We don't have enough to pay for what we've promised.

The government botched the program.

So when did we first find out about this? Last year? Five years ago?

Nope. We discovered the catastrophic flaws four decades ago! Ignoring for a moment that when Social Security (in the '30s) and Medicare (in the '60s) were passed there were dissenters pointing out the dangers, it was the early 1970s when the loud bells started going off.

What did we do?

Not much.

There were some adjustments, with taxes for Medicare and Social Security going up, but even in the early 1980s the government realized there was a long-term problem funding the benefits. The thing is, there's no political will to fix it.

This raises an interesting question. For 40 years, where have the recipients been? Where are the older, wiser members of our population, the very group that should be screaming for benefits to go DOWN? Shouldn't this group of people, in an effort to lessen the burden on their children and grandchildren, be demanding lower benefits?

Ha! Those people are few and far between. Instead, the whole idea that entitlement recipients should be working to have the payments reduced is seen as ludicrous. Who would turn down the money? Indeed, who would not demand more?

And therein lies the problem.

If I told a retiree that their Social Security and Medicare payments will come from the U.S. government, chances are he won't care too much. If I said the system is changed, and now they must collect it directly from their kids and grandkids... well, that would be more interesting.

Even though everyone knows where the money comes from, no one seems willing to connect the dots and then refuse the money.

It's understandable...

For all of their working lives the Greatest Generation (also known as the Bob Hope generation) and now the baby boomers have been told that Social Security (and later Medicare) is theirs... That they "paid in" and now they can "take out."

Of course nothing of the sort happened. These aren't savings accounts or IRAs. They are government-administered tax-and-spend accounts.

As we increasingly realize the implications of this situation we all understand the problem, but no one — and no group — wants to be the one to stop the madness.

So we all keep going, hoping that, as if by magic, the situation will correct itself. And every day we push a little more burden on to our kids' and grandkids' shoulders. But it's okay. It's just a little more.

While there is no "fix" for this on the horizon, you can help your kids and grandkids side-step at least part of the problem. Introduce them to tax-free or tax-deferred investing. Look to things like municipal bonds and insurance.

For whatever reason, people tend to think of these options as "old man" investments. But if trying to lower my tax bill — and take me out of the crosshairs of the IRS in the years to come — makes me an old man, then call me grandpa.

In fact, call me what you want, just take your hand out of my wallet to pay for an ever-increasing social burden.

"Thank Goodness Health Care Costs Are Contained" (And Other Idiotic Statements)

June, 2013

Recently the Medicare Trustees issued their annual report and — Happy Day! — it looks like the Medicare Trust Fund will not completely exhaust its assets until 2026, which is two years later than 2012's estimate.

I, for one, am sleeping better with this knowledge. I can stop worrying about the fact that Medicare is still going broke. I don't have to concern myself with the remaining 80 million-plus boomers barreling toward retirement and their Medicare eligibility.

Bankruptcy is 24 months later than last anticipated. Let's break out the champagne!

The reason Medicare is on such a fabulous glide path is because health care costs are rising at a much slower rate than anticipated.

Hmmm.

I have to think about that one for a minute.

This particular statement seems at odds with everything I see around me... and everything I hear from other people.

But maybe there's a reason.

Perhaps it has to do with what is seen as health care costs...

For the Medicare Trustees, it's represented by the cost of providing services. For me and the people I know, it is the cost of health insurance. When it comes to the latter, there's no containment. It's a moonshot of expenses.

Given our set up as a small business, I have an individual insurance policy. I carry my family of five on the policy and we have no chronic illnesses or pre-existing conditions. We have no on-going prescriptions. Our health issues tend to center around sports-related injuries, not illnesses. We don't smoke, don't drink to excess, and are well within our BMI (body mass index) numbers. In short, we're healthy.

Yet our insurance costs are climbing at double digit rates... and have for as long as I can remember.

We have consistently moved to policies that have fewer benefits and higher deductibles, to the point that we now use a Health Savings Account with a five-digit deductible. Even with such a low chance of us actually using any insurance funds to pay for care, our premium was $657/month.

I just received my premium notice for the next 12 months…

Our cost is going up by 13.8%, to $748/month.

This is with NO change in benefits and NO claims on which the company had to pay anything. And, this is before the Affordable Care Act.

But don't worry!

My insurance carrier, AETNA, sent a letter to let me know about the increase. It started the letter with large print stating: "Rates are going up — but we can help". The letter went on to tell me that indeed, my rates are going up, but that AETNA is looking for ways to keep costs down.

Unfortunately, when it came to "helping" me, the letter was uninformative. Under the heading "We're happy to help," the letter directed me to call my insurance broker, to log in to the AETNA website to learn about my plan, or to call the company directly. None of these seemed helpful, so I called to see what the representative would say.

When I asked about my plan going up by 13.8%, when I had claimed nothing, he told me that my cost had nothing to do with me.

That statement is both stunningly informative and unhelpful at the same time.

If cost has nothing to do with me, then how can I work to contain cost? Of course, I can't, which is the infuriating part.

I asked him if I should simply cancel insurance once the Affordable Care Act goes into effect, pay my $300 penalty per person per year, and then apply for insurance if I happen to get sick.

He told me that he had heard of the strategy before. And he wouldn't recommend it.

Genius.

I have no brilliant observation to give you today… but, as you and I both know, health care is a major cost that's not declining. It's increasing. And it's rising the fastest on small businesses and those who don't qualify for subsidized care (up to four times the poverty level, or about $80,000 per year in income).

So, once again, the exact people who are being asked to start businesses, hire more people, and spend more money are also being told they must provide more support for the economy as a whole.

Somehow these things don't compute…

But then again, I'm not a government bureaucrat. I'm sure that if I moved inside the beltway of Washington, DC, I'd immediately see how such a combination of things was best for me.

CHAPTER 7:
Commodities

There are long-term trends in commodities that drive long-term price movement. Growing wealth in populations can drive up the price of beef and chicken as consumers add more protein to their diets, while the increasing use of corn for ethanol, as mandated by the U.S. government, can propel that crop to dizzying heights. In energy, the shale boom in the U.S. is definitely changing the face of the energy markets — although not always in the way you might think. However, most of the trends in commodities are short term, driven by weather, crop yield, shipping constraints, etc.

And then, there's the "one." The one commodity that sells ads on CNBC and drives people to scream and yell. The commodity that frustrate so many because it just… won't… behave! It's gold of course, and chances are it won't do what you expect.

—Rodney Johnson

COMMODITIES

When It Comes to Commodity Prices...
Don't Confuse Weather and Climate

August, 2012

There's a raging argument about global warming. I'm not getting involved. Not because I don't have an opinion, but because I'm not informed enough to be very confident in my opinion.

But there's an aspect of the debate that I find interesting. That is, proponents of global warming now argue that the very hot weather we're experiencing across the U.S. is, NOT what they are talking about.

Their point is that we should not confuse weather — the monthly and even annual fluctuation in temperature and precipitation — with climate, which is of course much longer term.

And I find this interesting because that's exactly how we view the commodities markets…

We make every effort to separate the short-term fluctuations (weather) from the long-term trends (climate).

So while we obviously see many commodity prices high for the moment — like oil, corn, and even gold — we also see that the long-term Economic Winter Season will do its work, bringing these prices to heel.

Why is this the case? Because demand and the dollar will drive commodity prices lower.

The drop in global demand is evident as U.S., Chinese, European, and Indian manufacturing have all slowed in recent months. In the U.S. and Europe the numbers now point to contraction.

Manufacturing is slowing because of a decline in sales. So naturally, commodity producers feel the pinch as well. And as the demand for commodities slows down, commodity prices will fall.

There will be droughts, and there will be geopolitical scares, but these are short-term events. Long-term, the lower demand environment will push commodity prices lower.

As we've written many times, the U.S. dollar should keep moving higher. Already showing strongly against the euro, a move up against the yen and other currencies is next on the hit list. This isn't because the U.S. is doing so much right, but because other currencies have long lists of their own troubles.

The troubles in the euro are obvious.

In Japan, the problem is a very strong yen, which is crushing exports. And the lack of corporate growth is ruining the already limited opportunities for the young. The Bank of Japan has committed itself to a weaker yen, which must occur to give that walking-dead nation just a little more time on life support.

As for other currencies, like the Canadian dollar and the Aussie dollar, their economies are built upon the demand for commodities themselves. So as global demand for commodities slows, these countries will see their economies slow as well... and that will weigh on their currencies.

So what's the takeaway?

Should we all write-off commodities and leave these markets behind?

Of course not!

These markets are always quite volatile, which gives investors many opportunities to be on both the short side and the long side.

The thing to understand is that there is most likely going to be constant negative pressure in the commodity markets for the next several years. So do your best not to "fall in love" with any of your positions.

And most important of all, don't make the mistake of confusing "weather" for "climate."

Why Trading Gold for Oil Doesn't Make Gold Money

June, 2012

If India trades gold for oil, does that make gold money?

No.

Okay, it's more complicated than that, but the short answer is still: "No."

The long answer has to do with pricing and substitution, which are kind of boring words, and yet they're at the heart of the matter.

You see, while my accountant never fails to remind me that India's decision to trade gold for oil is a clear example of how gold can and will be used as a form of money, questions do arise, like: "How much gold is a barrel of oil worth?"

Hmmm…

To express the answer, I bet the Indians and Iranians aren't delving into the issues of consumption and production. Instead, they're probably looking to the international spot market and futures market, finding a delivery date and oil grade that matches what they're trading, and then using the price listed… in U.S. dollars… to begin their negotiation.

Then they're converting the U.S. dollars into ounces of gold, again using some international gold market that expresses prices in… U.S. dollars.

Gee. All of sudden the whole notion of trading gold for oil doesn't really seem like it gets too far away from the greenback.

To have gold truly perform the function of money, India and Iran would have to express the "price" of oil in ounces or grams of gold, and it would not be dependent on a U.S. dollar equivalent.

Instead, the rate of exchange would be dependent on factors such as how much oil is being produced and demanded in the world, and how much gold is available to exchange for oil versus other goods and services.

After all, that's how money works, right?

We determine the availability of the product or service in question, and then we determine how much of our store of U.S. dollars, or other currency, we want to use on that product or service.

The exact exchange ratio is determined not just by the transaction in hand (gold for oil), but instead is informed by all of the other transactions going on in the marketplace simultaneously.

Currently gold doesn't determine the price of the dollar; instead the price of the dollar determines the price of gold. So the precious yellow metal lacks one of the crucial requirements of "money."

Substitution is the other point that comes to mind when considering this exchange of gold for oil…

The Indians and Iranians made an arrangement that substitutes a commodity for money. Granted, the commodity in question (gold) has been used as money in the past, but it is NOT used in that way today. That is, it is not simultaneously a storehouse of value AND a unit of exchange.

So does the arrangement between these two countries satisfy the "unit of exchange" requirement? It would, if the two parties had not relied on the pricing mechanism I described earlier. Instead, all they've done is plug and play.

An example will clearly illustrate the point…

Really, They Could Substitute Anything

If the Iranians want to sell one million barrels of oil, the Indians would presumably look to the international markets and determine that the oil should cost one million barrels times the price per barrel of say, $90, which is obviously $90 million.

From there, the Iranians and Indians agree to substitute gold for U.S. dollars. To arrive at the right amount of gold, they divide the total oil price of $90 million by the price of gold at the time, say $1,550, to arrive at 58,064.5 ounces.

In this arrangement, the two parties could substitute anything. How about iPads? The $499 version? Instead of $90 million, or 58,064.5 ounces of gold, the oil now "costs" 180,360.7 iPads.

They could substitute wheat, ball point pens, tons of steel, Nikes… even hours of service in a call center. The Iranians could negotiate for a credit of say 18 million hours of call center service (assuming the service is priced at $5/hour), that some Indian company could perform at some time in the future. It could be in response to when Iran takes people into custody for no reason… their relatives could call 1-800-HOSTAGE to see what in the world is going on.

Okay, the last part is a bit extreme, but the point is made. Simply substituting a product or service in the place of money does NOT make that product or service the same as money.

So the Iranian/Indian arrangement, as proof that gold can be used as money, fails on two fronts.

But note, we're clearly stating that gold is not money TODAY. It has been in the past, and it can be in the future.

For gold to be money, a national government must recognize it as such, allow national debts to be paid in gold, and also use gold to pay for goods and services. That's not happening today.

For now, gold remains nothing more than a commodity.

What to Do: Buy Gold or Sell Gold

August, 2012

The Chinese have made a deal to purchase a large gold mining concern.

The Federal Reserve is making noises about another round of quantitative easing.

The European Central Bank (ECB) is working to — yet again — bail out everyone in the euro zone that needs bailing out. By all accounts, it must be time to buy gold!

By all accounts, except one: what happens next?

There's no question the Chinese are buying gold supply, but does that mean the gold price goes higher? Is China going to sell gold to the world or themselves?

In the past, the country has not shown an overwhelming desire to share. It's entirely possible that the Chinese take both their supply and their demand off the world market. Poof! In one move, one of the largest anticipated drivers of the price of gold is gone.

As for central banks… yes, there does appear to be another round of easing in the cards. We've forecast this for a long time. But just implementing the program doesn't ensure success.

The Fed and the others are trying to manufacture inflation. It's not working. The reason is they're busy focusing on liquidity and credit availability when the problem is excess debt and lack of demand!

Unless the Fed, the European Central Bank (ECB), the Bank of Japan, the People's Bank of China, and the Bank of England start printing fat stacks of cash and handing them out on street corners, with a mandate that the funds be spent, don't expect any greater results this time than the last… or the time before that… or the time before that.

In fact, expect less. Expect the markets to respond to the next round of quantitative easing with small applause and then a yawn. There will be a collective sigh of boredom.

There's a very real chance that the global economy, currently in the midst of a slowdown, will not be greatly affected by more printing.

The end result will be an overall compression of prices, which includes commodities and precious metals. As credit shrinks and economic activity slows, all metals, including gold and silver, should decline.

So what should investors be doing with gold? As the old saying goes: "Buy the rumor, sell the news."

Now is a golden opportunity… to SELL gold, not buy gold.

Use the current run in the "risk on" trade, which includes a run up in gold, to lighten your gold and silver investment positions.

Set a trailing stop loss, or use some other measure to lock in gains, and let the positions run a bit.

Does gold go to $1,700, or $1,900? We don't know, but we do know that right now, the stuff looks really shiny. It also looks ready for a fall.

That being said, this is not about your physical gold that was purchased as a hedge against calamity. We are often asked if we think investors should sell their gold coins. There's no way for us to know the answer, as each investor has their own threshold for how much gold makes them feel comfortable. But as for the holdings like GLD and SLV, it's time to plan your exit.

Who Should You Believe?

August, 2013

We recently received this question from a reader:

"You say that gold is going lower, but Edelson and others say that gold is going higher. Who should I believe?"

My first response was to ask, out loud no less: "Well who's going to tell you NOT to believe them?"

Larry Edelson, and others who preach a similar view point on gold, use sound logic. That is, the U.S. government is running huge deficits while the Federal Reserve is printing $85 billion per month. Historically, there are some examples of countries doing this only to destroy their currencies, leaving gold as the good bet. And there's no doubt these guys base their buy gold recommendation on exhaustive research.

Then again, so do we.

We don't take this position simply to be contrarian. Standing alone against a mob isn't fun. We, too, have done exhaustive research: decades upon decades of it, in fact. And in our view, gold is simply NOT all it's hyped up to be.

Naturally, we want you to believe us. Our arguments are compelling and logical. We've honed them through intense debate with our opposition. We practice what we preach in our personal portfolios and financial set ups.

But the reader's question is an important one, and one we see all too often. So here's an honest answer for him, and you…

Stop spending your time playing mental ping-pong and consider the situation.

For gold to shoot to dizzying heights, like Edelson and company believe, the U.S. dollar must fall dramatically. I don't mean the dollar must fall by 10% or 20%. I'm talking about a 50% to 80% drop here.

At the same time, investors and savers would have to believe that other currencies are equally risky, and then choose to hold a significant portion of their wealth in gold.

Keep in mind, this is a precious metal that you can't use to pay your bills, buy your food or secure a gallon of gas. It just sits there, gathering dust. It looks shiny, yes, but it still just sits there.

All of this would have to happen while the U.S. government — and other governments — did absolutely nothing.

Or, for us to be right that gold will remain muted and fall even lower, we need to see the U.S. dollar and other currencies remain relevant... and have our government and the governments of other nations remain intact.

Yes, they can devalue their currencies. They can work on solving their fiscal woes by taxing away more wealth. But as long as they stay in the game, then chances are the dollar, and other major currencies, won't die anytime soon.

Also, we still have that pesky situation of private credit contraction...

European institutions aren't lending and the U.S. credit picture is expanding only slightly because of student loans. The Chinese are lending, but it looks like a bubble that will pop.

Given this brief synopsis, take a few minutes and ask yourself: "Which one is more likely?"

If you still can't arrive at an answer, then use a different metric. Look up a chart of the price of gold for the last couple of years. You'll see a high of just over $1,900 and a current price of near $1,300. That should seal the deal.

As for me, well, I believe us, and I think you should too.

Gold's Worst Enemies

January, 2014

2013 was not kind to the yellow metal. While equity markets flew by 25% to 30%, gold fell by more than 25%. Ouch! That's going to leave a mark on portfolios across the country.

Investors who bought gold on its way down or simply held it after the top haven't seen a substantial reprieve in their current losses. It's entirely possible there won't be a letup anytime soon. The reasons are simple: gently rising interest rates and mild, if any, inflation.

As the Fed moves to taper its quantitative easing program and purchase fewer bonds — buying $75 billion instead of $85 billion — it's only logical that interest rates would go higher. After all, the biggest buyer on the planet has told everyone it'll buy less.

Interest rates moved up during 2013, and are still moving in that direction. This isn't true on the short end of the curve, where the Fed has pledged to hold down rates forever (or at least for the next two years), but it is the case for maturities longer than five years.

However, this doesn't mean that interest rates will fly to the moon…

Instead, I expect interest rates will gradually move higher by 0.5% to 1%.

That said, I do expect rates to fall back again with the next downturn in the economy, but that's a story for another day.

As for the yield on gold… well… there isn't one. As interest rates move higher, gold owners risk falling farther behind those who own interest-bearing securities and assets.

At the same time, inflation is more than just tame, it's downright house-broken. The Fed has printed more than $3 trillion over the past five years (an amazing amount!) and yet inflation remains less than 2%.

This is a testament to the deflationary forces in our economy, where wages remain under pressure and consumers continue to work down debt. This isn't a good thing for gold. The metal loves an inflationary run where the currency loses value. During times of low inflation, or even deflationary pressure, gold will naturally drift lower, just like other commodities.

Speaking of the currency, the two trends mentioned above — gently rising interest rates and very mild inflation — are the perfect recipe for a strengthening dollar. This gives investors confidence that their dollars won't lose a lot of purchasing power, while also attracting more investment because of higher yields.

Of course currencies and gold are generally mirror images of each other, so as the dollar strengthens, well… you know.

As I do every time I talk about gold, I will point out that I'm not talking about the gold people hold as a protection against calamity. Whether or not gold would serve a purpose in the event of a total financial collapse is debatable (how much gold do you trade for bread?), but I understand why people hold a certain amount in case of such an event. It helps them sleep at night.

Instead, I'm pointing out the risks of people holding gold as an investment, estimating the price will go higher so they can cash in for funds to use for other things.

While gold might bounce a bit (10% or so) from its current lows at this point in our economy, it appears that the trends are all going against the metal. Expect it to have another difficult year, no matter what celebrity spokespeople tell you on financial news networks.

COPPER

Thieves in the Night

July, 2013

There's got to be an easier way to make money than stealing air conditioners.

I mean, those outside compressor units are big, honking machines that are typically bolted to the concrete pads on which they rest. And yet, air conditioning theft is a common problem, particularly in states with large numbers of empty homes… like Florida.

People show up in the middle of the night, cut the connecting wires and hoses, and then haul those massive units away.

But they don't do it because they intend to sell the units whole. Nope, this is more like a chop shop that steals cars and strips off the pieces.

Air conditioning units are stolen because they contain an awful lot of what is now an expensive metal — copper.

And it doesn't stop there.

Thieves will also break into vacant homes and steal the copper wiring from the walls, and the copper tubing in the bathrooms and kitchens.

Unfortunately, sometimes the thief doesn't even break in. He simply uses his key, because sometimes homeowners will gut a home before they give it back to the bank under a foreclosure.

It's not pretty, but it happens.

It didn't used to be like this. Then again, copper wasn't always expensive.

The red metal is a key ingredient in building, particularly in plumbing and wiring. As the construction market heated up in the U.S. and around the world in the 2000s, copper moved higher in price, up from about $1 per pound to more than $3 per pound. Along with increasing prices came increasing incidents of theft. It's easy. All you need to steal copper is a few tools, a strong back, and the ability to haul it away.

Then came the downturn…

After 2008, the price of copper fell dramatically, back below $2 per pound, as all types of building ground to a halt. The sudden stop in construction sent shudders through many of the commodity markets.

However, the resulting central bank actions sent the metal back up again, a move that was exaggerated by the rebounding Chinese economy, where copper is both an industrial metal and a storehouse of value.

You see, in China, a person or business can pledge copper as collateral for a loan. This double use — a storehouse of value and as an input in construction — gave the copper market quite a boost after the financial crisis, elevating the price of copper... even as building in the U.S. and Europe dried up.

The price of copper soared back to nearly $4 per pound. The result was a lot of expensive copper in empty homes and a lot of people out of work... a recipe for vandalism and theft!

But lately the price of copper has fallen back down to earth, settling in the low $3 range. This is strange because it comes at the same time that the U.S. housing market has bounced back a bit, with many people (not us, mind you) calling for a rapid rise in new construction.

With such a tailwind, how could copper fall in price instead of marching higher?

Again, it is all about demand in Asia.

While there is still massive construction taking place in China, the pace has cooled somewhat, so the demand for copper has cooled as well. At the same time, the Chinese government has taken aim at a financial shenanigan that holders of copper commonly engage in, called rehypothecation.

That is a fancy way of saying: "Loan it again, Sam."

In the financial world when something is pledged as collateral it is hypothecated. To rehypothecate is to take something that has been pledged to you as collateral, and then pledge it as collateral to someone else for your own loan.

The danger in this is immediately clear.

If a ton of copper can be pledged as collateral for a loan, or hypothecated, and then rehypothecated for yet another loan, then it's possible that an infinite number of loans could be based on a single ton of copper.

If any single borrower defaults, then the copper is removed from the system and every other loan is called. If two borrowers default, then one of the lenders will be left high and dry because there was, and remains, just a single ton of copper.

The Chinese government is working to cool the hypothecation — and therefore the rehypothecation — of copper, so it's limiting the ability to use the metal as collateral. This is causing a slowdown in the import of copper because much of the internal supply can now be sold to end users instead of being tied up in collateral arrangements.

At the same time, there have been a series of reports showing weakness in Chinese manufacturing. Given the varied industrial uses of copper, such a slowdown would certainly mean less demand for the metal. The fact that China is responsible for 40% of the world's copper consumption makes this a big deal.

The end result of all this is that copper should trend lower in the weeks and months ahead as the collateral trades unwind and the slowdown in Chinese production works through the system.*

This is bad news for countries that export copper. And, of course, it's bad news to people who steal air conditioners in the middle of the night.

* Since this article was written, copper moved from $3.10 per pound up to $3.30, and then fell to $2.90.

Why Oil Will Never Hit $200 a Barrel

April, 2012

Oil is going to $200 per barrel. Or is it $300? I forget.

Then again, I don't agree, because I know something about oil that many seem to overlook. That is, oil is its own worst enemy.

There are many reasons why the price of oil is moving higher at the moment, including central banks around the world printing money with abandon, the stable demand for oil that is a combination of falling U.S. demand and rising demand from developing nations like China, and geopolitical concerns about Iran, Yemen, Syria and others.

All these things drive the price of oil up. But there is a counter-force at work with the price of oil… something that will prevent oil prices from ever reaching the $200 mark.

This counter-force doesn't come from the oil companies, or political parties, or even car manufacturers as they try to foist electric cars on us.

No. This force is closer to home.

This force is you and me — the end-user of oil and oil-based products. And it has a name — self-limitation.

You see, oil — or better yet, the rising price of oil — is a self-limiting commodity. The higher the price goes, the more motivated, and the more likely, we are to use less of it.

When gasoline reaches $3.50/gallon, and marches toward and then over $4.00/gallon, we begin looking for ways to curb our consumption. We begin to batch our driving errands, trying to get as much done as possible in one trip. We park the big cars. Suddenly, the gas-guzzling, high-profit, big pick-up trucks sold by domestic car companies stop selling. None of which is surprising. After all, consumers today are very price conscious, particularly now, right after the greatest economic downturn in a generation.

While not math geniuses, we're able to figure out that spending more on gasoline, while not getting any greater use out of it, has a detrimental effect on our standard of living. When more of our money goes to filling up the tank, we have less to spend on eating out, going to the movies and drinking beer.

I might be wrong, but I'm pretty sure most red-blooded American males would rather drink their beer and drive a Chevy volt that uses electricity, than hang on to their Chevy Suburban and have to give up the beer. Being a Suburban owner, I can attest to this.

If We Stop Buying, They Stop Selling

Oil's self-limitation doesn't stop with the end user. The main suppliers of oil get just as upset when the price is too high, because they recognize the predicament.

In 2005, then-President George W. Bush made U.S. energy independence a plank of his State of the Union address. In the U.S., the speech was a yawner, but around the globe, oil-producing countries were outraged that the U.S. President would be so bold as to lay out a unilateral energy policy.

You see, if we start buying less oil, then the oil companies start selling less of their product. And if we buy less oil because we're moving to other energy sources not controlled by energy producing countries, then we, as customers, are lost to them forever.

When all you produce is oil and sand, you try to protect your oil business in any way you can. And runaway prices that drive off customers who will then never return is very, very bad for business.

Oil might spike now and then. There might even be good reason for the price rise. But don't buy into the $200/barrel scare-story. The forces fighting against such a price spike are simply too strong.

NATURAL GAS

The Bigger the Grill… The Bigger the Boom

March, 2013

My high school raised money regularly. We had bake sales, car washes and raffles. Of course schools in other parts of the country had raffles as well, but ours were special.

We raffled off BBQ grills.

Not your typical, tear-drop shaped grill. Not even the bigger, square grill with a big lid… nothing that you'd find at a Lowe's or Home Depot.

No sir!

I'm talking about a man-grill. A double-decker, diamond plate steel beast…

You see, I went to high school in Louisiana, southwest of New Orleans (yes, there really are towns south of New Orleans), where the entire world revolved around supporting the oil industry.

If you had a truck and some skill with welding, you were almost guaranteed a good paying job. And from time to time, the local high school would ask you to build a grill to be raffled off.

This became a point of pride for the builder, so the grills got bigger and fancier.

I'm guessing there are a lot of high schools today in the Dakotas that are getting grill donations, because they certainly have the oil boom… and all the joys and pains that go with it.

Currently, rent in Williston, ND, a town at the center of the recent oil boom, is around $2,000 for a one-bedroom apartment. This is four to five times the cost of a similar unit in Fargo, ND, or even the cost of the same apartment in Williston five years ago. The town's ability to increase the housing stock is far behind the demand for space as people flood the town.

At the same time, the unemployment rate for North Dakota is just over 3%, which is less than half the national rate. These two simple statistics should be bringing one word to mind: OPPORTUNITY.

The situation in North Dakota is being repeated near most of the major shale oil finds around the country, in areas around the Dakotas, Texas, Louisiana... even Pennsylvania.

As U.S. companies have developed efficient ways to extract the gas, oil, and other fuels, the regions that support these operations have become hotbeds of economic activity and growth. And the companies and towns involved in the long-term support structure for these industries, mostly based in Louisiana and Texas along the coast, are busy preparing for the eventual export of fuels on a level never seen before.

The migration trends of the U.S. have been dramatically affected by the shale oil boom, reversing the flow of people out of North Dakota and intensifying the migration into states like Texas. I can't overstate the knock-on effects of this.

Yes, welders will have jobs. So will construction workers, store clerks, waiters, restaurant owners, administrative workers, teachers, high school coaches, landscapers... you name it.

When a large migration happens over a short period of time, there's plenty of pain at first, such as extremely high rent, but then the services necessary to support the migration are built. Given that this movement of people is focused on energy, which our country needs, and is eager to stop importing from people that hate us on the other side of the world, it's hard to imagine this trend slowing down anytime soon.

So while there might be limited opportunities in Jacksonville, FL, or Detroit, MI, it doesn't mean there are no opportunities available around the country. Just as there are busts, there ARE booms. And the shale oil boom is bringing with it the largest migration of people and cash-register of business opportunities of the decade.

Natural Gas — The Future of Energy

June, 2012

I must admit, I thoroughly enjoy a good old American road trip.

We're lucky. My children are good travelers. They take the ups and downs of long hauls in their stride. We've logged up to 850 miles in a day, but typically we try to limit ourselves to 500 miles a day as we crisscross the country. It is not uncommon for us to rack up 3,000 miles in the course of a week, as we explore the best of what America has to offer.

Along the way I've come to anticipate the all-important question: "Where's the next bathroom?"

When there are five people in the car, coordinating bathroom stops can be a marvel of linear programming. Usually we try to combine bathroom breaks with food and a fueling stop, which leads me to the heart of this article...

While the truck stop, Pilot Flying J, has been around for almost half a century, my family and I didn't start visiting it until we happened into one when we found ourselves overflowing and running dry (so to speak).

What we found was reasonably priced gasoline and the treasure of all road trips... clean restrooms! This meant that, where possible, the Pilot Flying J stations moved to the top of our list.

And now I have another reason to extol Pilot's virtues: The company is partnering with T. Boone Pickens' new enterprise, Clean Energy (CLNE), to provide compressed natural gas (CNG) refueling stations in over 100 locations.

This is the missing piece to the energy puzzle.

The last ten years have been weird for energy. Oil spiked higher. The U.S. has been involved in two wars in the Middle East. Green energy has been praised and subsidized. And natural gas went from severely limited availability to a 100-year supply thanks to fracking.

So now what? In the end, it all comes down to ease and price of conversion on the part of users. ⟋

When it comes to electrical generation, plant operators can develop a fuel supply that services many, be it coal, gas, hydro, etc. Those of us who simply "plug stuff in" don't really notice.

But when it comes to vehicles… well, that's a different story.

Not All Fuels Are Created Equally

Ethanol was great if you grew corn. But if you ran a vehicle then the agri-fuel was hard on your engine and had inferior energy storage. You simply can't get as much energy out of a gallon of ethanol as you can gasoline. In addition, the production of ethanol uses a lot of energy AND the industry is widely subsidized, including mandated use as a fuel additive.

Bio-diesel is an alternative, but we can't use it in large quantities (meaning greater than 5% to 15% of a fuel mixture) in newer cars because it "gums up" the works.

Electric vehicles are tethered to recharging stations and suffer from a lack of power and range.

This is where compressed natural gas-powered vehicles enter the fray. You see, it's relatively inexpensive to convert a gasoline vehicle to a CNG vehicle; just a few thousand dollars. And there's no loss of power or range.

And with the new over-supply of natural gas, a gallon of CNG only costs about $1.50 while traditional gas costs around $3.30. That's a 55% savings — pretty good if you ask me. With ease of use, no loss of power or range, and a great price point, what we're missing is availability. The Clean Energy/ Pilot Flying J partnership is large step toward bringing CNG vehicles into the mainstream.

I couldn't be happier with this transition. Not only are CNG vehicles cleaner burning, and therefore better for the environment, but the fuel source is local. The current account deficit of the U.S. would plummet if we cut our daily oil imports in half. At the same time, we would boost employment in the U.S.

Here is a fuel source that can exist side by side with petroleum — same fueling stations, equivalent power, basically same engines — that we can produce locally to cut our imports, cut our costs, employ more people and reduce, if not eliminate, our dependence on nations that would like to see our demise.

The only things in our way are infrastructure build-out and consumer awareness. As we overcome these two problems, the increased use of compressed natural gas will help carry the U.S. into the next period of economic prosperity.

It won't occur overnight, but be thankful that we're on the right path in this part of our economic evolution!

And if you need a clean bathroom on a long trip, don't hesitate to park among the big rigs at a Pilot Flying J.

Natural Gas vs. Gasoline — Which Would You Pick to Fill Your Car?

September, 2012

There's a point in the movie *Other People's Money* when Danny DeVito's character — Lawrence Garfield — explains to a group of workers that their company will go out of business, no matter how good they are at their jobs.

He yells that even the best buggy whip maker went out of business as cars became the norm…

It makes me think of shorthand, which they taught in high school for years… or secretaries…

Personal computers wiped away some of the main functions secretaries once performed. Things like the creation and receipt of memos, files, mail. Shorthand left the building for the same reason.

These are all clear examples of creative destruction.

That's where a new technology or process displaces the old. It causes short-term pain… even displacement. But in the long-term, it leads to a better standard of living for the world.

And such advancements can come quickly in tough economic times. Because that's when companies try to save money to survive. That's when consumers seek out ways to stretch their dollars.

That's what the U.S. now faces… a number of new creative destruction junctures in different industries, including energy…

The word fracking has gone mainstream, even though it still shows up in red when I type it in MS Word. The term is short for fracturing and refers to the process of hydraulically breaking up rock formations underground to release oil and natural gas.

This process has vastly increased the amount of recoverable natural gas and oil in the U.S., which will lead to an energy boom in the years ahead.

I have no doubt that this is creative…

The wave of energy supply, particularly natural gas, is bringing about innovation in natural gas powered engines for cars, trucks, you name it… This could significantly cut the amount of emissions created in the U.S. while lowering the cost of operating vehicles.

There's also a wave of innovation in the refueling arena. There are a large number of consumers that already have natural gas piped to their homes, so it's possible to refuel a natural gas car at your house.

Which brings up the destruction part...

The guy at the corner who sells gasoline is already feeling the pinch of high-mpg cars and hybrids. If consumers can refuel their vehicles at home through existing infrastructure, then even fewer of these stations will be needed.

And fewer gasoline tanker trucks will be necessary on the roads.

The move to the new technology has great potential to lower costs, improve quality of life and generate jobs. At the same time it will displace an old technology, leading to the decline of certain support businesses along with the associated jobs.

Such is the process of creative destruction.

The key insight is not to dwell on what is lost, but to look for the opportunity in what is gained.

ENERGY

The Pain and Gain of Renewable Energy

October, 2013

Every month, at about the time I get my electric bill, I wonder why I don't install solar panels. Our region of the country receives ample sunshine, and because of our southern location we have long days in which to capture energy from the sun.

Then I remember why I've not taken that step yet. The darn systems are so expensive! Well, they used to be.

Over the last decade the cost of solar power systems has halved, and that's before you take into account the value of subsidies and tax credits. Still, it's hard to justify installing solar power at my home, given our falling energy use as the kids go off to college.

But I'm not the prime target of solar power installations.

In fact, given the upfront costs and the reality that spreading those costs over more real estate pointing to the sun is better, retail consumers in general are not the prime target of solar power installations.

It's all about businesses. More specifically, it's all about businesses that have really big physical footprints.

As recently reported in *The Wall Street Journal*, Walmart has installed 65 megawatts of solar capacity, while Costco and Kohl's have installed 38.9 megawatts and 35.6 megawatts, respectively. The more capacity they install, the more they control their own energy generation and cost. As the price of solar power (and other renewable fuels) declines, this move makes companies that benefit from generating their own power look even smarter.

On the other side of this trade are the traditional power companies that used to sell electricity to Walmart, Costco, et. al. These power companies are the heavily-regulated, electric generation businesses that also sell power to homeowners and small businesses across America.

As the large corporations cut the proverbial cord — or at least shrink it — they leave the traditional power companies with less revenue and fewer clients. What typically doesn't decline in such a scenario is the need and even legal requirement for the traditional power companies to maintain their electrical generation equipment and all of the physical lines over which that power is distributed.

So on the one hand there are big companies making intelligent choices about how to manage their power needs and how to better contain costs. On the other hand there are electric companies that must continue providing certain levels of service and safety, even in the face of falling revenue.

Hmmm.

I think I see a problem here… and potentially a fall guy.

As power companies lose large commercial clients, they'll have to find some way to make up the revenue. The first and only place they'll turn is to their remaining clients, which of course are homeowners and businesses that were too small or too slow to install alternative power sources.

It's more than conceivable that while our country transitions to a balance between on-site generated power and the traditional delivery from large companies that there will be a cost of maintaining the old system. A cost someone will have to pay.

Residential clients, the consumers least likely to move to alternative energy, are the ones that will foot the bill.

While this should raise alarms for homeowners, particularly those in areas like southern California where companies are quickly ginning up onsite power generation, it should also make investors scan their portfolios for investments that might be vulnerable to these trends.

The problem children of stocks include electric utilities, which tend to pay dividends. Retirees seeking income often hold such stocks.

That said, there are a couple of bright spots (no pun intended) here, beyond the obvious of harnessing a renewable energy source. As companies purchase more of this equipment the expertise involved in installation and management increases while the cost falls.

There's also something here for those entering college. The fact that we are once again dispersing the ability to generate power means there'll be a wide array of companies looking to hire employees who are knowledgeable about power generation, power distribution and system maintenance.

In 10 years it's possible that companies, from grocery stores to shopping malls, will employ small departments of engineers and technicians with such expertise. For anyone sending a kid to college, this could be a path that provides quality employment for decades to come.

Investors Counting on This One Commodity Could be in for a Rude Awakening

January, 2014

Back in 2005, everyone was worried about U.S. jobs moving overseas. When I spoke to groups, someone in the audience would inevitably stand up and ask if I thought this issue was a long-term problem for us. I always answered "no." But not for the reasons they might have thought...

I would go on to explain that the U.S. was facing an ugly downturn in 2008 to 2010... one that would put almost all economic opportunities on ice. This would slow the move of jobs from here to anywhere.

Usually my audience met this answer with skepticism. That was okay. I was used to it. Still am.

But I was wrong... at least, in part.

The economic downturn arrived on schedule, and jobs stopped drifting overseas. In fact, for a couple of years jobs simply stopped. The problem of long-term unemployment reared its ugly head and has been with us now for five years.

But along the way, something else happened. Unexpectedly, electricity got cheap thanks to fracking and the low cost of natural gas.

Now we face a situation where wages have fallen for half a decade and energy costs are low. This combination is driving a trend of job re-shoring, where jobs previously sent overseas are being brought back home.

For example, Whirlpool is adding about 100 jobs to its plant in Clyde, Ohio, where it makes washing machines. This move is expansionary. The company is not cutting production at its facility in Monterrey, Mexico, to increase production somewhere else. It's simply growing its Clyde facility. And it's a move that's indicative of how companies are viewing the competitive position of the U.S.

When it comes to heavy or breakable items, manufacturers place a lot of emphasis on the distance from the point of production to the end retailer.

As costs in the U.S. spiraled higher during the 1990s and 2000s, the savings that producers could achieve by building in foreign locations trumped that problem of distance.

The current trend of more competitive U.S. wages and dramatic savings in energy are reversing this equation. For many items, manufacturers are finding it cheaper to produce here than to produce overseas.

This is good for our economy, but it comes with caveats.

Today, U.S. auto manufacturers plunk out millions of more units than they did in the 1970s, yet they employ tens of thousands fewer people. The reason is automation.

Even though the cost of employing people here has fallen, there's no question that labor is still expensive. But the cost of automation keeps falling. So manufacturers are constantly on the lookout for new techniques and processes, for automating tasks that speed up production, lower error rates and reduce the cost of labor.

While jobs are coming back to the U.S., I wouldn't say we're seeing a manufacturing renaissance that will suddenly bring millions of jobs back home.

Compounding the automation issue is the low cost of electricity. Those robots need juice. While natural-gas prices are quite low today, at about $4.40 per mBTU, we don't expect them to remain there.

The U.S. recovers abundant amounts of natural gas through fracking, but as of yet, it doesn't export the fuel beyond Mexico. To get the gas farther from our shores we must liquefy it. Three plants have been approved for this process, but none are on line yet. The first is expected to open in 2015.

As the U.S. gears up to sell natural gas in the international markets — where prices are as high as $19 per mBTU in Asia — it's only logical that our prices at home will increase, and could potentially double.

Then what happens to the math that made production at home more attractive? It's entirely possible that the equation gets turned upside down once again.

Any investor — from the kinds who play with equities to those who manufacture stuff or hope to find work in the industrial space — who is counting on cheap energy for the next decade, particularly from the likes of natural gas, could be in for a rude awakening.

CHAPTER 8:
Real Estate

This sector is vital to the overall health of the economy for several reasons. As a point of consumption, homes typically represent the largest item that most people will ever purchase, and the transaction is usually done with 80% credit. In other words, for every saved dollar a person spends, he is borrowing four more.

On the employment side, the skilled labor necessary to build a home typically commands solid, middle class wages. As the housing sector grows, so does the middle class. However, as housing languishes, so does the middle class.

And then there's the investment front. Over 70% of Americans consider the equity in their home as part of their retirement fund. Setting aside for a moment that if a person sold their home to access the money, they'd still have to live somewhere, this means that people are exceptionally interested in the value of their homes!

Putting these three things together — consumption, employment, and investment — it's easy to see how real estate is one of the most important sectors in our economy. You could say our lives revolve around it.

—Rodney Johnson

REAL ESTATE

The Opportunity in the Housing Market is NOT a House

September, 2012

Many years ago, my wife and I went to the public library. We were young, newly wed and broke… so the public library was a great resource.

She walked away with several sci-fi books and thrillers. My stack included a book on monetary policy in Romania in the 1950s. Granted, it wasn't a page-turner, but I did find it interesting.

Obviously my taste in reading material is decidedly non-fiction and technical, but every once in a while I need a break. When that happens I turn to a great source of humor and fantasy — the National Association of Realtors (NAR).

In the world of fiction, the National Association of Realtors is one of the best writing groups in the world. For five years this group has continuously pumped out reports that show the housing market is at its cyclical lows, a screaming buy and on the verge of a turnaround that will astound and amaze!

The only thing left for people to do is buy, buy, buy! Then… of course… nothing happens.

So has the housing market bottomed?

We don't think so, but even if current house prices prove to be the lows, the chances of a wildfire run in the price of homes seem remote at best.

We just came out of a decade where the availability of cheap credit drove home prices and the number of units sold to lofty heights. Who expects that to return? No-one with any grounding in reality, that's for sure.

Instead, what has occurred is a reality check that continues to frustrate the NAR but makes perfect sense to everyone else.

The pendulum has swung from a government- and bank-induced focus on home ownership, that treated shelter like a can't-lose investment and ATM, to a more reasonable approach that treats housing like what it is, a place to live.

In this new normal, where sanity prevails, people ask themselves all sorts of interesting questions like, "Can I afford this home?"… "Do I plan to live in this area for many years?"… "Is my income safe?"… "Is this home worth the price?"… and the all-important, "Do I want to be tied down to a home right now, given the state of the economy?"

As you might imagine, many times the answer to one or more of those questions is "No!"

New home sales are roughly half of what is considered "normal," while existing home sales are about 20% lower than what the NAR thinks they should be.

But all those people have to live somewhere, and there aren't that many friends' couches up for grabs or parents willing to take back aging kids and their spouses, children and pets.

That's why the bulge in the marketplace is in rentals… and it is not showing signs of slowing down.

We've discussed this trend many times in our research because it's a result of two larger trends driven by demographics.

First, consumers that would have been home buyers in earlier years are shying away from that market. This leads to a tremendous increase in demand for rentals.

Second, investors searching for yield will find this market and invest in the streams of rental income. This is what drove us to identify an apartment REIT last year as a good investment for our *Boom & Bust* portfolio. This REIT is now reporting 97% occupancy and expects to drive up its rental income — and subsequent payout to shareholders — this year.

The point is that, just as our publication names imply (*Survive & Prosper* and *Boom & Bust*), there are two sides to every market. If you are flexible enough in your outlook, you can adjust to the changing facts on the ground and join the growing trend instead of being run over while you hang on to what was the best choice for yesterday.

…Unless of course you are writing forecasts for the NAR, which, to remain relevant, must hang on to the notion that everyone wants to be a homeowner.

For the rest of us, if you're interested in a good dose of fiction, you can probably find these NAR reports in your local library.

Saying "I Told You So" Can be so Satisfying

March, 2013

If you have daughters, you know the one big drawback.

It's not the expensive weddings. You can plan for those. It is not the boyfriends. You can scare them witless (which is quite enjoyable).

No, the main issue with daughters is much closer to home. In fact, it's IN the home. It's the bathroom.

Once girls hit their teen years, the bathroom becomes an extension of their lives. From clothes to cosmetics to hair products, the place is in shambles at all times. For the life of me I can't fathom how they can trash that particular room of the house so quickly and so thoroughly.

It's different with boys. They're messy, no doubt... but there aren't all of the other products that are sprayed on, smeared on and otherwise left as residue around the room.

Frankly, I try to avoid my daughters' bathroom at all costs. Physically and verbally. If I ever mention the state of affairs in there I get the typical teen response (said in a shrill voice): "Why were you in there?!"

The fact that I pay for that bathroom (and everything in it) doesn't sway them in the least.

Now, sharing a bathroom with one of your children as they age can be difficult. Sharing one with another adult, long after you got past the age of roommates, can be a nightmare.

But this is what many U.S. households look like today...

It's called multi-generational living...

The dreaded call can come anytime. An adult child who has been living and working on his own for years is now out of a job and will soon lose his ability to live independently. Or maybe it's the other way around. It could be a parent that has lost a steady paycheck and simply has no idea what to do next.

Whatever the circumstances, the outcome is the same... one generation moving in with another. Welcome to a world of sharing you never expected.

The situation has become so ingrained in our population over the last five years that now home builders are cashing in on it. Lennar Homes is promoting what it calls "Next Gen" homes, which it describes as having a "home within a home." From its own promotional materials:

Each NEXT GEN suite includes a separate entrance, living room, kitchenette, one-car garage, laundry and private outdoor living space. Lennar designed this unique floor plan to be incorporated into the main home floor plan in a way that allows it to be a separate space but also offers direct access from the main house, depending upon the family's needs.

Hmm. That sounds nice, right? We're all just gathering together but get to keep our "space."

The reality of the situation is elsewhere in their material:

Studies show that one of out of six people already lives in a multi-generational household and that by 2020 there will be an overwhelming trend for this type of living space.

What they don't say is that many of those people are currently living together for economic reasons and there is no light at the end of this tunnel.

This trend came out of the financial crisis, but that doesn't make it bad…

Once in a while we should ask ourselves why we do things the way we do. I can gripe and complain about my daughters' bathroom, or joke about how I don't want my parents moving in, but does it really have to be that every single person has their own home?

This idea of independent living for 20-somethings, empty-nesters and retirees is a very American idea. One that seems more to the benefit of real estate professionals than anyone else.

While it was a difficult economy that brought us back to multi-generational living, maybe we're better off because of it.

If the Next Gen homes by Lennar do well, it will be interesting to see what happens to all of those rosy forecasts of a real estate revival. After all, much of the hoped-for recovery depends on those multi-generational families taking the first opportunity to split up again. This is just one more reason to be very cautious about the path of residential real estate.

McRibs and McMansions

June, 2013

I love McDonald's Big Macs… and don't get me started on the fries. I can almost taste them now!

With that being said, I can't remember the last time I ordered either one of those things. In fact, the only time I go to McDonald's is to grab a quick drink (for $1, who can beat that?) or for breakfast when we're traveling.

As I get older, the taste of McDonald's food has not gotten worse, but it now wreaks havoc on my waistline and makes me feel ill for hours after eating it.

Talking about McDonald's like this makes it sound like a restaurant, which is how it started and how it advertises itself to this day. But if you look at the operations of the business, it is something else entirely.

As one person put it, McDonald's is really a large commodities firm that sells to the end consumer… and what a big buyer of commodities it is! The Super-Size retailer buys more than one billion pounds of beef each year, and more than three billion pounds of potatoes, which gives McDonald's the ability to influence these markets in a meaningful way.

However, these are consistent markets for McDonald's, meaning they buy these commodities every year. In other markets, McDonald's comes and goes, dramatically affecting prices, production, and supply. A great example of this is the McRib…

McDonald's introduced that weird slab of sauce-covered pork in the early 1980s because the McNugget was so wildly popular. As the company ran out of chickens, it needed something else to satisfy demand. Enter the McRib.

The pseudo-pork sandwich (that includes bits of heart, tripe, and stomach, to help it keep its shape) was not a great seller, but it developed enough of a following to be a re-occurring offering for the chain.

This means that McRibs — and therefore McDonald's demand for pork — comes and goes. As you might imagine, the pork market reacts accordingly every time McDonald's puts the McRib back on the menu.

This isn't to say that pork doesn't have a market beyond McDonald's. It obviously does, but the entry and exit of such a large player is big factor…

which is why the recent stories about the housing market remind me of the McRib.

Housing has a cycle based on demographics, which cheap credit and the overall health of the economy can accentuate. In addition, the entrance — and exit — of large players can affect the housing market.

This is the concern today…

Just like pork buyers and sellers who witness McDonald's driving their market, those in real estate are watching large hedge funds and other institutions push around home prices and supply.

For the last several years, multi-billion dollar firms have been buying up single family homes with the intention of renting them for a while and then disposing of them through sale or securitization (bundling them up and selling them to other investors).

Because this was happening at the bottom of the housing market cycle, the entry of such large players lifted prices and shrank supply more than it probably would have in normal times.

Anyone who was buying alongside these investors has benefited from the notion of a rising tide lifting all boats.

Anyone who was interested in buying but has not yet pulled the trigger probably feels left behind about now because of how far prices have risen in the past eighteen months. But an interesting thing is happening on the way to the closing table. Some big investors are backing away.

Blackrock, the biggest and best known firm involved in this business, has purchased over 26,000 homes and still appears to be going strong. Others, such as Och-Ziff and Carrington, have ended their purchases for now, in September 2012 and April 2013 respectively. The reasons they gave centered on the rising home prices and how that affects their long run profitability.

Which brings up what this means for everyone else…

If several of the large institutions that were buying single family homes, at what they believed to be cheap prices, have slowed or stopped their purchasing, what does that mean for prices going forward?

Yes, there will still be home buyers, but just like McDonald's in the pork market, a major player (or several major players) will be absent. Without a substantial increase in purchasing from other sources, this development should, at the least, be a note of caution to other real estate buyers, if not an all-out warning sign.

The last thing you want to be in the real estate market right now is either a seller holding out for a higher price or a buyer that just got into the market right before the big guys left. That could leave you with a queasy stomach and a little sauce on your face.

We see warning signs all around in the housing market, and continue to warn investors who have recently become landlords that trouble is possibly ahead.

A Mortgage From the Mob

March, 2013

Mark Twain once quipped that "Truth is stranger than fiction." His reasoning was that fiction must stick with possibilities, whereas the truth has no such limitations. He was right.

We all know we had a debt crisis fueled in particular by sub-prime home loans. Those loans, made to people with less than stellar credit histories, ended up taking on all shapes and sizes. There were interest-only loans, No Doc loans (where you did not even provide your credit history), piggy-back—no-money-down loans, and of course the famous NINJA loans, where a borrower didn't have to show income, a job, or assets (No Income, No Job, No Assets... NINJA).

Rightfully, all of these things faded into our past as we dealt with the aftermath of the housing bust, which laid bare the problems such loans caused. You would be forgiven for thinking that such things could not... WOULD NOT... rise from the ashes.

And you'd be wrong...

There is indeed a new type of loan out there... it doesn't require a credit history and it has a unique feature. It's secured not just by the property, but also by a life insurance policy on the borrower. How cool is that?!

FastFunds Financial created this new mortgage, which it says doesn't require a personal guarantee or a credit check. All of which leads me to believe FastFunds must be run by the mob. Who else could be that ingenious when figuring out how to protect their investment?

The logic is pretty straightforward really...

If the home goes up in value and/or the borrower makes his payments on time, everyone walks away happy. Problems only arise if the home falls in value and the borrower fails to make good on his debt. At that point, the lender, FastFunds in this case, has the 10% down payment as a hedge against a loss on the property. But what if the loss is bigger than that? What then? Well, because the mortgage is guaranteed by a life insurance policy, the answer seems obvious.

The mob will send a guy with a name like One-Eye, or Tiny, or Pretty Pete, to "encourage" the borrower to pay. If the borrower fails to make good, then he might suffer a terrible accident and end up "sleeping with the fish," wearing a pair of cement shoes. Brilliant!

Who needs foreclosure? Who needs to robo-sign documents? Short Sales are a waste of time! FastFunds doesn't want your stinkin' personal guarantee, they want their money! If the cost of making good on the loan is the ultimate sacrifice by the borrower, well, so be it. Along the way there would be a huge cost savings by cutting out the lawyers and all that court time.

All kidding aside though…

It would seem that the debt crisis is still so fresh in people's minds that they're reluctant to snap up any sub-prime mortgage product, regardless of any twists added. But FastFunds has an answer for that. It's targeting people who specifically have credit problems.

Arguably, this group has few options for getting a mortgage elsewhere, as they have proven in the past to be a bad risk, yet they still want to own homes. The big question is, should we be encouraging that? Is our growth in housing so weak that we need to go after not just marginal buyers, but those with proven bad track records, to fuel growth?

I don't really think the mob owns FastFunds, or that the company would take out a hit on a borrower to get their money back, but I do think the sort of loan offering they have on the market can only end badly.

Unfortunately, when mortgages become a mess and end badly, it is usually us, as taxpayers, who end up paying.

We've Resorted to Fighting Over 3/2/2s

May, 2013

One morning, several years ago, I was running late for a TV interview. I had just finished up a radio interview and realized I had twenty-five minutes to get to the on-location site for the live TV spot.

The topic was housing.

The location was an empty field.

Well, it was almost empty. It was a new neighborhood with streets, sidewalks, and streetlamps… but no houses. I drove (too quickly) to the location, hopped out of the car, walked up to my mark opposite the reporter, pinned on the mic, and the interview started.

After the real estate bust it was clear to everyone that we were not going to simply revert to cheap credit again anytime soon. For housing to rebound at all, something had to change… and it did.

There has been a seismic shift from owning to renting, which was a huge opportunity for those that had the ability to buy property and rent it out. I say "was a huge opportunity" because this play has already been squeezed for the easy profits. What is left behind at this point is the stuff that takes work.

Right now, investors of all sizes are locked in a battle over homes with three bedrooms, two baths, and a two car garage… otherwise known as a 3/2/2.

As the housing market rolled over and foreclosures exploded, there were suddenly a million different coaching classes available on buying foreclosures and turning them into rental property.

Granted, when things were darkest in late 2008 and early 2009, this was a gutsy thing to do, but as the economy stabilized the investment made sense. Banks and other mortgage lenders were convulsing over loan losses and property was being sold at very low levels.

Real estate prices got so low that annual rents represented more than 10% — and often more than 15% — of the cost of the home. During a time of record low interest rates, where else can an investor get that kind of return?

Of course, this situation attracted a lot of small investors, and eventually a lot of really big ones as well…

The investment group Blackstone has spent over $3 billion to buy 20,000 homes, becoming one of the largest landlords in the country in the process. At the same time, Colony Capital has raised more than $2 billion to do the same thing. These amounts are small compared to the size of the housing market, but they show a sizeable trend in how institutional investors are now getting involved in, as well as shaping, the housing market.

From March 2012 through March 2013, home prices in the U.S. were up more than 7%. But rental prices on single family homes were up merely 0.1%.

In many cities, the two measures (home prices and rents) moved in opposite directions...

In Fort Lauderdale, FL, home prices were up 10.7% while rents were down 1.2%. In Phoenix, AZ, home prices shot up by 24.2% while rents increased by a measly 0.3% (less than the rate of inflation). The spread was the widest in Las Vegas, NV, where home prices moved up by 24.6% and rents fell by 1.9%.

Given the two trends of rising sale prices and flat to falling rents, it's clear that the marginal return of buying a home to rent it out is declining. In short, this is becoming a crowded trade, where everyone is doing the same thing.

At what point do homes become too expensive to justify the buy-to-rent strategy?

The answer is somewhat different for each investor, because everyone's cost of capital and tolerance for loss and illiquidity is different. I'd imagine Blackstone can take a deeper loss, and suffer longer illiquidity, than most individual investors.

So the key to this market is shifting from merely buying the property right to including a clear exit strategy. The days of buying cheap homes on the courthouse steps and then renting it out while it appreciates dramatically are over.

If you're in this market, or considering getting in, be very careful of any assumptions made about price appreciation. The housing market has been driven much higher in the past two years by investors both large and small, taking out the easiest profits. Whatever you buy at this point could be in your portfolio a lot longer than you anticipated.

The New Drug Dealers on the Block

March, 2013

The recovery in the U.S. housing market has gotten a lot of attention lately. The government reported that January new home sales surged to an annualized rate of 437,000 units, which is up from roughly 300,000 at the bottom of the market.

Interestingly, this move was not mirrored by the sale of existing homes.

Sure, there has been an upswing, but nothing like what has occurred in new homes. So I began wondering why this might be the case...

To make this divergence more interesting, new homes now cost 37% more than existing homes, which is the largest gap since this measurement began back in 1968.

If new homes cost a lot more, why are new home sales picking up faster, particularly in an economy marked by flat and falling wages?

I didn't have to look very hard to find the answer...

New home builders are now drug dealers.

It is not that every new home comes with a mirror full of cocaine or a bale of marijuana in the basement. No, for my purposes the drug is not a substance ingested to create an altered mental state. Instead, it is an obligation assumed to create an altered physical state.

The name of the drug is debt... and apparently we are still addicted.

We want our homes and we don't care what cost we inflict on ourselves, or our fellow citizens, to get it.

People want homes but cannot afford them. They have declared bankruptcy in the past few years, or have other "blemishes" on their credit reports. They have been turned down by lenders. The situation is difficult, and more than just a bit of a pain to deal with.

Then they walk through new home models. Home builders talk about how they can smooth out the process of getting a loan, easing the burden of the buyer. This all sounds great, so people buy new homes.

Brilliant!

But as usual, there's more to the story.

Home builders are in the business of building and selling homes. The pool of qualified home buyers has shrunk dramatically in the last six years because lending standards have returned to some level of reality and consumers are in a worse financial position. These two things are at odds, so home builders took the obvious path…

They began "assisting" people with mortgage qualification like never before.

Home buyers are put through builder-sponsored credit counseling in order to help repair their credit reports. Builders have associated mortgage companies that help buyers apply for FHA- or VA-backed mortgages, which require little in the way of down payment. Want to use a monetary gift to make a down payment? I bet a home builder can show you how!

Amazingly, all of this is leading people to purchase new homes instead of existing homes. Along the way, buyers are buying more home than they otherwise would have, at the highest price in history when compared to existing home stock.

Hmm…

So home builders are relying on sales to marginal buyers who have trouble qualifying for loans in order to boost sales. Along the way, the home builders are making great use of government-guaranteed mortgage programs, which puts the burden of default on taxpayers and requires little down payment on the part of the borrowers.

This is the good news everyone is so giddy about?!

Did we learn nothing from the housing meltdown?!

Call me crazy but this does not sound like the beginning of a flourishing market to me. Instead, it sounds like a story with a predictably bad ending. And it's one more reason you should avoid home builders at all costs.

I Want My Lousy T-Shirt

March, 2013

When you live in Florida you learn things.

Much like understanding that when Congressmen get to Washington they can no longer do simple math, in Florida we know that when tourists get to our sunny state they can no longer function well in society.

They seem genuinely surprised when a cashier at the grocery store presents them with a bill… they have to dig for their wallets as if they thought the goods were going to be free. Then they go on to explain they are from another state, where I guess grocery stores don't charge for things.

When it comes to driving, tourists seem to go at about half the posted rate of speed, particularly over bridges. I have no idea why this is the case, I just know that it is.

In addition, I know that many tourists also lose their ability to make rational clothing choices. How else can you explain beer hats — hard hats that hold cans of beer and have two-foot straws for drinking — and t-shirts that read, "I'm with stupid"? I'm pretty sure that anyone wearing such a shirt is not only proclaiming their friend's lack of intelligence, but also their own.

I might hate most of this kitschy-wear, but it was one of these shirts that came to mind when I read about the much vaunted recovery in housing…

The classic tourist shirt reads, "My grandparents went to (fill in the blank) and all I got was this lousy t-shirt." The wearer of the shirt wanted — and expected — so much more! Maybe a light up pencil, or a flamingo yard ornament… now that would have been cool. Instead, he or she simply got a shirt.

If only we were so lucky.

The Fed has spent trillions of dollars to create a recovery in housing, hoping to goose the economy through spending and employment along the way. Recently we've been inundated with the news that housing is indeed bouncing back, solidly moving higher and clearly on its way to the moon!

Really?

The report that seems to have so many people excited is the new home sales report, which showed sales in January to be at an annualized rate of 437,000 units, which is far above the recent low of about 300,000 units, but still over 60% off the peak.

However it's not the distance from here to the old top that catches my attention. It's the "at an annualized rate" part of the description. In reality, only 31,000 new homes were sold in January. If this number is multiplied by 12 we would produce an estimate of 372,000 homes, which would be the "annualized rate" from January. However the U.S. government seasonally adjusts this number to account for the typical trend this time of year.

We know how seasonal adjustments typically pan out…

They are the same things that led the government to tell us gasoline was 0.3% cheaper in January when in reality prices were 3% higher!

So to see if the government's estimate of a blistering housing recovery is correct, I looked at other things that should be rising at the same time.

In terms of employment, our economy lost over two million jobs in construction from the top of the market to the bottom. So far, we have only recovered about 200,000 of those jobs, or 10%.

As for GDP, private residential construction adjusted for inflation fell by more than $580 billion, or about 55%, from the top of the market in 2006 to the bottom in 2011. Since that time we have added back roughly $66 billion, or about 11%, of what we lost. That's not much of a recovery.

Even on the private side, where there is much fanfare about the housing recovery, some of the numbers need closer inspection. Pulte Homes reported a $206 million profit in 2012, which is good, considering the company lost $2.3 billion in 2007. This pales in comparison to the company's gain of $1.4 billion in 2005.

All of this brings me back to the notion that the discussion about a resurging housing industry in the U.S. seems a bit premature. I know the Fed has spent $2 trillion in order to push housing higher. I know the Fed has held interest rates to historic lows to keep mortgages cheap. I know the federal government keeps handing out cash through government-guaranteed loan programs to give people an even easier path to borrowing.

But so far, the numbers that matter — employment and GDP contribution — just don't add up to much.

And it gets worse…

The Fed's efforts have been fueled through the printing of money, which lowers our standard of living. It's also been fueled by their ability to keep interest rates artificially low, which removes our ability to earn any return after inflation without risking the equity markets.

To top it all off, 90% of all new home loans originated today are backed by taxpayers through FNMA, FHLMC, FHA, or the VA, with the FHA and VA programs requiring small down payments. So any new round of foreclosures or write offs from another down draft in housing will fall squarely on us as taxpayers.

It's like the Fed went on a binge (holiday) to push this industry higher, and we didn't even get a lousy t-shirt. In fact we got no gift at all.

It's not very satisfying.

Welcome to the Newest Iteration of the Mortgage Mess

July, 2013

Say your neighbor Joe wants to borrow $1,000 from you. He's willing to provide security for the note in the form of his car, and will even sign a promissory note that is his personal guarantee, pledging all he has in order to pay up. You and Joe come to terms on interest, and a deal is done.

But a few payments in, Joe stops sending you money.

You call him out on it and point out that he owes you these funds or you can legally take his car... and by the way, he has made a personal guarantee on the note.

Then you get a call from the Mayor of your town. It turns out the Mayor has heard about this private deal and that Joe isn't paying what he owes. You might find it odd that the Mayor is involved, but you might also be comforted to know that other people will show up to encourage Joe to pay his debts.

You'd be wrong.

In this instance, the Mayor is worried that if Joe loses his car, then he won't be able to make it to work. This might jeopardize Joe's employment and could even lead to Joe paying less in taxes.

With less income, Joe will support fewer businesses in town.

By paying less in taxes, Joe is causing the city to fall behind on its revenue goals. This is very concerning to the Mayor, so he wants you to cut Joe's note in half. It's obvious Joe's not good for entire amount anyway, so you might as well reduce the value of the note so that Joe can once again become current and everyone will be happy.

Everyone except you, of course, because you will lose half the money you lent to Joe.

So you choose not to. If by some stroke of luck Joe starts earning more money, you might actually get back what he owes you. And you could always take his car and try to recoup your money that way.

This displeases the Mayor, so he threatens to sue you. His goal is to compel you to sell the city the note for 50% of its value, thereby hanging you with the loss.

How on earth can the Mayor do this? By claiming imminent domain, and that reducing the value of Joe's note by 50% is in the public good.

Welcome to the newest iteration of the mortgage mess.

Several cities on the West coast are contemplating this exact sort of process. Their goal is to confiscate, through imminent domain, the notes on underwater homes by paying the current note holders less than face value.

This leaves the loss with the current lender, and sounds like a fabulous way to fix the mortgage problems facing millions of homeowners... except for one thing. It flies in the face of contract law and the defense of private property, two principles on which most everything we do in the U.S. is based.

The lenders, who would be forced to eat losses in this scenario, did not force borrowers to take on mortgages. They don't stand to profit from any gains a borrower might realize on the property purchased. They simply offered credit to willing buyers.

This is not a defense of banks. I'm not shy about expressing my utter disdain for a lot of banks and how they did — and continue to do — business. If a bankster broke the law, he should be punished. If they're gumming up the works by holding up modifications, throw them in jail.

But the reality is most of these mortgages are not held by banks. Instead they're held by pension funds and trust funds as parts of large pools of mortgages.

What exactly did a pensioner in Indiana, whose pension fund happens to own a mortgage-backed bond that contains properties in California, do that should make him the bearer of forced losses?

The groups that are pushing this approach have many good reasons for doing so. Most of the homes they're targeting would be in foreclosure eventually, where lenders get even less money.

The process for servicing mortgages makes it impossible to get a clear representative for the lender, mainly because the loan has been broken into pieces and sold to many different people, so there is no way to negotiate with the other side.

The homes, if they're empty, become a blight on the neighborhood.

Financially-troubled homeowners are trapped between two impossible choices: Keep paying for a losing asset or walk away and risk credit destruction.

These all make sense, but they are trumped by one thing. This is private property that involves a willing agreement between two parties. Each borrower took on a loan and promised his full faith and credit to repay it, along with pledging the property as collateral.

And this isn't like one homeowner stopping the construction of a freeway. This is actually the reverse. Instead of one home, or one contract, this is hundreds and thousands of contracts that would have to be seized, all in the name of serving a large, undefinable purpose.

If such a thing were to happen, how could it be limited?

If the public good is an amorphous cloud of betterment for society, then any and all contracts, personal property, and even lifestyle choices are on the table. Local governments would gain the right to mandate or prohibit whatever they felt served us all, and leave financial losses at the feet of whatever party they choose.

The risks here are clear... and getting bigger. While this imminent domain fight is taking place out west, the CFPB (Consumer Financial Protection Bureau) is busy writing regulations in DC that will require anyone lending money to verify that the borrower is in a comfortable position to take on a loan, or else the lender can be held responsible for failure to repay.

If you own part of a bank, invest in banks, or have any dealings with the extension of credit, be forewarned. The years to come look fraught with danger as regulations and litigation overwhelmingly turn in favor of the non-paying borrower.

This Choice IS Important

March, 2014

The Federal National Mortgage Association (Fannie Mae) is an interesting animal.

The government agency was started during the recession of the late 1930s to help banks make more housing loans.

The basic premise: Fannie Mae would buy mortgages from banks, who could then re-lend the money.

Only, Fannie Mae was much more generous than banks were.

Instead of offering the typical five-year loan, with a required down payment of nearly 50%, Fannie Mae would buy loans that had a 30-year term and a down payment of 20%... and then it would charge an insurance fee to cover any losses.

These terms, along with a borrower's good repayment history, became known as "conforming"... that is, they conformed to what Fannie Mae wanted.

Fannie Mae wasn't generous with its own money, because it technically didn't have any. The entity was funded by selling bonds. The loans and small insurance premiums then backed the bonds.

The question is: Why would investors who bought Fannie Mae bonds be happy with the new terms on offer to borrowers when banks weren't comfortable with them?

That's a good question.

Everyone assumed that the U.S. government backed the bonds Fannie Mae was selling. The problem was that the government only guaranteed a paltry $25 million, even though Fannie Mae eventually had trillions of dollars in loans outstanding.

Fannie Mae went public in the 1960s, and threw off lots of dividends to equity investors, interest to bond investors, and bonuses to management.

Things were great... right up until they weren't.

Fannie Mae, along with its sister company Freddie Mac (FHLMC), went bust in the summer of 2008.

The money coming in from home loans during the dark days of the financial crisis, along with funds from the insurance premiums, simply weren't enough to make good on all the bonds outstanding. So the U.S. Treasury put the two companies into conservatorship.

Not bankruptcy, mind you. Just conservatorship. The ultimate hole in the balance sheet was $180 billion… just a touch above the government's $25 million guarantee… but that was okay, because the Treasury announced it would make all bondholders whole.

And *that's* when the world of bond investing changed.

The U.S. Treasury's decision to fully back the bonds of the two housing companies, which were both private entities by that time, even though they started as government agencies, effectively nationalized the firms.

Any debt they incurred was a de facto debt of the U.S. government.

Voila!

Fannie Mae and Freddie Mac could issue *any* amount of debt they wanted to and buy *anything* they felt like, because repayment from underlying homeowners didn't matter at all.

Uncle Sam would pay, as was made clear by the $180 billion cash infusion.

During the crisis, and in the years since, Fannie and Freddie, along with the Federal Housing Administration (FHA), have backed over 95% of new home loans.

The explosion in demand for Fannie and Freddie funds meant that the two companies received an enormous inflow of insurance premiums being charged on new mortgages.

This led to a dramatic increase in revenue for the two companies, and a quick repayment of the $180 billion that taxpayers provided in 2008 to bail them out.

This all sounds good, but keep in mind what happened…

Fannie and Freddie were only able to continue operations because they were *bailed* out.

Then they were only able to borrow *more* money to buy home loans because now they had the explicit backing of the U.S. taxpayer.

These are not private companies. They are effectively agencies of the U.S. government.

When the U.S. government takes on the responsibility for your debt, both past and future, people will lend to you freely, but their willingness to give you money has NOTHING to do with you. It has everything to do with the government's guarantee.

Now we have to decide what to do with Fannie and Freddie. Their stock is still traded, and they still have the structure of private companies.

Should they be fully nationalized and operate like the Federal Housing Administration (FHA), or cut loose?

The choice *does* matter.

If the entities are sent along their way, then they shouldn't carry the backing of the U.S. government anymore, which means their ability to borrow freely and cheaply will be greatly diminished.

This would drive up the cost of mortgages and slow down the housing market.

On the other hand, if the two companies are fully nationalized, they become pawns in the political game, where political motivations drive decisions about lending (lend more to that group over there, lend less to this group over here, etc.).

Indeed, some of this went on before 2008.

We want to avoid a repeat of the previous situation, where the companies made private decisions and earned private profits, but in the end, we as taxpayers took the losses incurred.

This falls into the category of privatized profits and socialized risks.

Unfortunately, it's the most likely outcome.

Congress doesn't want to actually nationalize Fannie and Freddie because the government would then have to assume all of their risks, and show their liabilities as outstanding on its balance sheet.

While the rebound in housing and the increase in the insurance premiums have repaired their corporate balance sheets, another drop in housing could cause more damage, as well as losses.

At the same time, these companies were effectively the lenders of last resort for home mortgages during the depths of the crisis, so no one wants to stop the money flow for fear of creating a new crisis in housing… or making another downturn worse.

Without clear direction for these two entities, Congress gets to have it both ways.

It can keep money flowing in from bond buyers who rightly believe that the U.S. government backs all bonds, and keep the assets and liabilities of the two entities from appearing on the country's books.

Of course, this fools no one.

No matter what Congress says, or in this case, doesn't say, everyone knows who's on the hook for future losses: U.S. taxpayers; the REAL payers of last resort.

Blood for Vampires

October, 2013

I like to know things. I read non-fiction for fun and I'm constantly on the lookout for facts and figures that border on fringe.

While this can sometimes lead to odd dinner conversation, it also makes me better at my job. I get to bring readers like you information and analysis that allows you to make better-informed decisions… hopefully very profitable decisions.

Unfortunately, there are times when I have to let people know that their assets are being stolen from them… and that there really isn't much they can do about. In fact, the current financial system is designed for this theft to occur.

But that's not where today's story begins. Instead, it starts in housing…

For years we've talked about the overhang of homes that banks foreclosed on and now own. There are millions of these units simply sitting in inventory, going nowhere.

Our view was that eventually this inventory would be sold, leading to a flood of houses hitting the market, which would potentially spark the next down leg in housing. After all, what else would a bank do with an empty, foreclosed home? Surely they have to sell it, right?

Well, not exactly.

In fact, about half of the foreclosed homes are not even empty.

Realty Trac recently reported that 47% of all bank-owned, foreclosed homes are currently occupied by… wait for it… the previous owner.

So a person who lost a property through foreclosure — a person who has no legal interest in the property and no debt to repay — is now living in the home for nothing.

In Virginia, previous owners occupy more than 70% of bank-owned foreclosures. In California the number is 55%.

Now, a good question might be: If the bank foreclosed on the previous owner and took away the property, why is he still living there?

The answer appears to be: Because it serves the bank's interests.

Right now banks have way too much of this type of property. They would love to get rid of it, but just like anything else, if they flood the market with inventory then prices will fall.

This would hurt the rest of what the banks have in inventory and it would hurt their efforts to pump up their mortgage businesses. After all, would potential homeowners be rushing to buy if they saw a lot of "For Sale" signs in yards and prices dropping?

Banks have done the logical thing: They have driven up prices by keeping supply off the markets, thereby supporting their own business lines and protecting the value of their inventory. That's why these homes are called "vampire properties." They're sucking the life out of the housing markets by constricting supply.

While this inventory is off the market there is the pesky problem of upkeep…

If a bank owns 1,000 homes, it must mow the grass, keep the bushes trimmed, and keep everything in working order. As every homeowner knows, houses require constant attention to little things so they don't turn into big problems.

Maintaining 1,000 homes is a tall order. So instead, a bank can simply allow the previous owner to live there, hopefully maintaining the property. It's a win-win for the banks and the previous owners, while it's definitely a loss for current home buyers.

But this is only half the story.

While holding inventory off the markets to keep prices high might make sense, it certainly leads to the question of how banks can afford to do this. Where does the money come from to fund this activity?

The answer is: from savers.

The Federal Reserve sets interest rate at which banks can borrow funds from one another. This is called the Fed Funds rate. While this rate fluctuates a bit with market gyrations, it tends to stay close to what the Fed wants.

Today, the Fed Funds rate is 0.00% to 0.25%. So when a bank either has excess capital at the Fed that it can lend, or needs some uncollateralized capital for a day or two, the interest rate on the transaction is a paltry 0.25% or less. Keep in mind this is an annualized rate, so the real amount of interest charged is miniscule.

The Fed Funds rate is what drives all short-term interest rates, and therefore is the driving force behind the rate of interest financial institutions pay savers on deposit accounts.

A quick check of Bank of America's website shows that the bank is paying 0.01% interest on all savings accounts, no matter what the balance. In short, banks pay nothing, even though inflation is running 1.5%.

At the same time, banks use our deposited money to make loans and to buy securities. A 30-year mortgage from Bank of America will cost a highly-qualified buyer roughly 4.25% in interest, while a 10-year Treasury bond yields 2.62%.

If a bank simply keeps its excess reserves at the Fed, it'll still earn 0.25% in interest.

There's nothing wrong with banks earning more from lending or investing than they pay out in interest to depositors. The difference between the two rates of interest is called the spread and it's how banks make money.

Instead, the problem is that the Federal Reserve is holding the Fed Funds rate at historical lows levels simply to boost the profitability of banks. It is this profitability that gives banks the leeway to hold these millions of properties off the housing market.

Higher profits flow to banks, previous homeowners who lost their properties to foreclosure enjoy mortgage-free living, and savers are drained of their assets.

While vampire properties might be sucking the life out of the housing markets, vampire monetary policy is crippling the savers of the nation.

But at least the banks are profitable.

DEBT

Squatters Blow Mortgage Money on iGadgets

March, 2012

Bank of America has come up with an exciting new plan to turn non-paying home owners into upstanding renters.

Okay, that's a bit sarcastic, but it is true… and along the way Bank of America takes back ownership of the home.

The idea is to change the model from deadbeat homeowners to renters, so the property can be magically transformed from a home teetering on the brink of foreclosure into a solid, income-producing rental that Bank of America can sell to investors.

Fannie Mae and Freddie Mac, who previously tried a similar program, are now in discussions to sell large pools of foreclosed homes to investors planning to turn them into rentals. There is one condition. These investors must promise not to sell the foreclosed homes they acquire for at least three years.

Make no mistake. This will have a tremendous effect on consumption.

A Downgrade From Squatters to Homeless…

The movement of mortgage delinquencies through the system, and the mass sale of foreclosures into the rental market, is going to push the down-and-out people squatting in their homes onto the street.

Stories of homeowners who have quit paying their mortgage are everywhere.

But what do these people do with the cash they save by not paying their mortgage, property taxes, insurance payments or any rent? I think it's a safe bet to say they're not diligently socking that cash away. It's more likely they're spending it on iPads or iPhones, on dinners out or new cars.

As the programs at Bank of America, Fannie Mae and Freddie Mac go into effect, those people living in these homes for free will have two choices — pay rent or leave. And even if they leave, they'll have to pay for housing somewhere.

All this points to consumer spending slowing abruptly ahead. The economic indicators that have been modestly positive lately — like retail sales and consumer confidence — will rollover. As they do, there will be ample opportunity for investors who are short the markets (equities, bonds, etc.) to make substantial gains.

Make sure you're ready.

The Lunacy of the Current Mortgage Market

January, 2014

The Federal Reserve (and much of the financial press) is betting on the return of one of the worst economic deals in the world. That is, allowing people to borrow 80% of the money they need to buy a home and then repay that debt over 30 years.

Who in their right mind would lend such money?!

As it turns out, the answer is (almost) no one. That's why the U.S. government created the Federal National Mortgage Association (FNMA, or Fannie Mae) and eventually the Federal Home Loan Mortgage Corporation (FHLMC, or Freddie Mac)… and why these programs or something similar will be with us for a long time.

In the years before the Great Depression, home mortgages were straightforward…

A borrower could take out an interest-only loan for 50% of the purchase price and the balance was due in five years. That's it.

The typical thing was to roll over the unpaid balance of the mortgage at the end of the five years.

Of course, when the Depression hit and mortgages came due, banks either didn't have the capacity or the stomach to roll over these loans, so they simply called them. And since the borrowers didn't have the funds to pay off the loans in full, homes were foreclosed and sold, helping to drive the property market into a tailspin.

Franklin Delano Roosevelt recognized in the 1930s what the Fed recognizes today… that home building creates a bunch of jobs and new money through credit extension, so he was eager to get the residential housing sector back in action.

Unfortunately, banks were still smarting from the Depression and weren't all that eager to make new loans. The idea of lending money to people who might lose their jobs, against assets that could drop dramatically in value, seemed risky.

So FDR did what many government officials do. He supported a program that makes little economic sense to address an immediate economic concern. In 1937, Fannie Mae was born.

The years between the creation of Fannie Mae and its bailout in 2008 were filled with both monotony and excitement. There were times when nothing happened, and there were years when new tweaks goosed the creation of mortgages and therefore spurred the housing market.

Through it all, it's clear that the politicization of the mortgage industry can have disastrous consequences. And that raises a question...

If lending money for 30 years, to people who can (and do) have dramatic changes in income, against assets that can (and do) change dramatically in value, is a risky proposition, then why do we continue to do so?

Because in the eyes of the U.S. government, we must.

Fannie Mae or Freddie Mac back almost all of the mortgages written today, allowing banks to get them off their own books almost immediately. In a time of tepid economic growth, wage deflation and rising interest rates, who wants to make, and then hold onto, a 30-year loan? No one. Which is why no one else does it.

Now, when I say "no one else does it," I mean no other country operates this way. Other nations use adjustable mortgages, typically on a five-year term, and with some sort of government backing to keep the banks happy.

With all of this said, one thing is clear: The U.S. won't go cold turkey in dismantling or otherwise closing up Fannie Mae and Freddie Mac. The economic cost of doing so in terms of a slowdown in the real-estate market would be simply too painful.

But I'd imagine that it goes even further. The economic cost of doing ANYTHING —taking any step, making any change — to make U.S. mortgages more sane (shorter terms, higher down payments, all adjustable) will never happen because politicians control the decisions. And no politician wants to be seen as responsible for diminishing the economy or a market in any way.

Just when it seemed the situation couldn't get more surreal, the Fed came along and began buying up almost every scrap of mortgage-bond debt available through its quantitative easing efforts.

So now taxpayers get the joy of knowing that not only are they still on the hook for dubious mortgage programs, but they are also financing those mortgages by having their saved dollars nicked every time the Fed prints more money to buy the mortgage bonds that back the loans!

You just can't make this stuff up.

RENT SECURITIZATION

Blackstone Wants Your Money

November, 2013

I didn't grow up in a house full of keen shoppers.

Like most Americans, we were payment buyers. The goal was to make sure that whatever we bought on credit — cars, appliances, etc. — resulted in monthly payments that didn't exceed the monthly paychecks.

Of course, we racked up debt, but hey, the monthlies were affordable.

From time to time this led to purchases that seemed attractive at first, but in hindsight were obvious mistakes.

It took me over ten years of financial education, both personally and professionally, to move beyond this way of thinking and truly gain control of my financial situation. Maybe I'm a slow learner, but eventually I get there.

Once I was in the driver's seat, things changed rapidly…

I viewed every purchase from a different stand point: utility, possible years of service, alternatives, ways of achieving lower overall cost, etc. This made shopping for big ticket items more of a hassle because we had to do so much legwork ahead of time, but in the end it has paid off in spades, particularly when it comes to big items, like cars.

Years ago we needed a new car, so I went into research mode.

After identifying the makes and models that fit our goals, we went for test drives and eventually settled on one that fit our needs.

Then began the purchase process. Over the next month I located fourteen dealerships that sold the vehicle we wanted and got the contact information for the sales managers.

Then I paid a data service $49 to send me the actual sales information for my zip code as well as surrounding areas for our chosen vehicle.

Armed with this information, I waited until the end of the month and then sent a note to every sales manager outlining the price I would pay for the exact vehicle I wanted. The first one to respond would get my business.

It took less than an hour.

After getting to the dealership, the transaction took less than 45 minutes.

The salesman explained that they view people as "units" or "profit." Both are goals of dealerships, so if a dealership hasn't pushed out enough units in a month they are more inclined to sell to people like me.

Interesting.

So if I do my homework, come to the table armed with knowledge, and wait until the seller has a need for a buyer like me, then things work out. Otherwise I run the risk of getting fleeced.

This lesson has been applicable to many things, including investments like bonds.

Often people get persuaded by what appears on the surface. They don't delve too far into the mechanics of how the investments work.

This is what got the world into trouble with mortgage backed securities (MBS) during the housing boom. Now this same persuasion seems to be happening again… with a different type of bond.

Blackstone is now selling bonds backed by the rental payments made for single-family homes.

Hmmm.

Over the past several years large investment firms have been snapping up single family homes to turn them into rentals. Blackstone on its own has purchased more than 30,000 homes across the country.

These firms stepped into a broken real-estate market and used their cash to get good deals. The goal was to buy the homes cheap and create streams of income through the rental payments, as well as cash in on the eventual appreciation in the value of the homes.

Now the whole buy-to-rent trade has grown long in the tooth.

Home values have moved higher in the last two years, but incomes have not. This means that affordability — for both buyers and renters — hasn't improved. In fact, it's gone backwards.

At the same time, our economy is facing long-term headwinds that should keep people on the move when it comes to employment.

None of this bodes well for long-term rentals.

And this doesn't' even contemplate the operational issues that such a setup would face. Who manages the properties? What happens when properties are damaged or just sit empty? Are the bonds backed by the value of the homes, and if so, what happens if home values and rents fall together?

The entire enterprise sounds like a mismatch. Investors hand over their money for the long term (the time horizon of the bond), but the only visibility they have on returns is short term.

Blackstone is selling $479 million worth of these bonds. I'm sure that when they hit the market they will be a hot item.

Chances are they'll offer an interest rate that yield-hungry investors of all sizes will find irresistible.

But that doesn't make the bonds any less risky, just more likely to persuade buyers who aren't doing their homework.

When it comes to buying bonds backed by rental payments, it looks like investors will end up being the providers of "profit" to the selling investment firms, which is a trade that could look pretty foolish in hindsight.

CHAPTER 9:
RETIREMENT

It's fitting that the last chapter in this compilation is about retirement, because it's the last chapter of life, and yet it still has no end. There's no agreement on when it should be, what should be included, and how it should be funded. We have an existing system in Social Security that is broken it relies on more young people paying into a system that funds older people.

Now that our demographics (there's that word!) are inverted, the system doesn't work. So it must change. And therein lies the rub.

Do we lower benefits or raise taxes?

I'm not sure the answer will be finalized before I reach retirement myself! But I do know that I need to pay attention, because the direction of the debate could be lower benefits for me, higher taxes for me, or — unfortunately, most likely — both!

—Rodney Johnson

RETIREMENT

Demographic Trends: The Revenge of Retired Baby Boomers

September, 2012

We have two offices in Florida. One in Delray Beach and one in Tampa. So, from time to time I drive along the Interstate that runs from Tampa, through Orlando, to the East Coast.

One of the sights along the way is the Airstream Ranch in Dover, which consists of seven Airstream travel-trailers planted vertically in the ground. (Yes, this is real... just Google "Airstream Ranch" to find a picture.)

Now, I must admit, I have an affinity for the shiny Airstreams because those torpedo-shaped travel-trailers bring back memories from my youth. But the industry in general — travel-trailers and more importantly RVs — represents something else altogether.

I call it the revenge of the retired.

Think about RVs, those colossal vehicles that seem like mobile homes with engines. People well into their retirement years are driving these vehicles around with nothing more than a standard issue driver's license.

If you drive up to an RV lot in a two-door hatchback with enough credit or cash, you can drive out in a vehicle that is probably bigger than the house you grew up in.

What makes most RV drivers qualified to make such a leap? Absolutely nothing. And now the roads are about to fill up with these behemoths, with their aging owners behind the wheel...

Seven years ago, in a different publication, I wrote about the rise of the RV and travel-trailer industry based on demographic trends in the U.S.

While the bulk of baby boomers are now firmly in their saving years, the leading edge of the generation is already retiring. As time goes on, the trickle of retirees will become a flood, which will in turn fuel all things retirement-related.

Like RVs.

While it might seem out of step with the mainstream media push toward fuel efficiency and conservation, the sale of large RVs (that have little regard for fuel efficiency) is already on the rise.

$4 gas? Who cares?

Diesel higher than gas? Doesn't matter.

There are sites to see, grandchildren to visit and little granola-eating, yoga-doing soccer moms in Toyota Priuses and Nissan Leafs to run off the road!

As Boomers force their way through the gates of retirement they will explode this market, just like they did for Harleys in the '90s and 2000s. This explosion will bring with it a demand for ancillary or support products and services.

Not coincidentally, down the road from the Airstream Ranch on I-4 is Lazy-Days, an RV park, repair center, hotel and spa where RV'ers can get their home-on-wheels serviced while they relax in comfort and style.

Seeing the opportunity ahead, Wal-Mart announced a plan, years ago, to let RVs park in their parking lots overnight, because they provide a secure, well-lit parking place and a chance to sell supplies.

The point is that even though our nation is aging, it doesn't mean all areas slow down. Some industries will see a tremendous increase. The key is to see the changes coming before they happen so that you can take advantage of the opportunity. Or, as in the case of RVs on the road, you can get out of the way as fast as possible!

When It Comes to Your Retirement... Math Can be Painful or It Can be Enlightening

October, 2012

Mean... median... mode... dispersion... reversion to the mean...

Are you asleep yet?

For those who don't like math, I understand that equations and computations can take on the appearance of nothing more than squiggles on a page, a seemingly endless drawing with little rhyme or reason.

Fair enough. Not everyone is mathematically inclined.

Unfortunately, everyone has responsibility for funding their retirement, and it is here that math can be your friend or your foe.

The good news is that the concepts involved are simple... the bad news is that many — including those who are supposed "experts" — screw it up all the time. The problem, you see, is understanding average versus sequence...

A common refrain in the world of investment self-help is to advise investors that over the long haul stock markets go up and the U.S. markets earn around 8% (on average).

Well, obviously if the U.S. markets earn an average of 8%, then they MUST be going up, or else the long-run average would be zero or less than zero. So let's focus on this concept of average.

The notion of average is simple. Add up all the data points and then divide by the number of data points.

If the city of Tampa gets just over 36.5 inches of rain in a year (365 days), then the average rain fall per day is 0.1 inches.

Easy.

But does this mean that every single day the people in Tampa should expect 0.1 inches of rain? Of course not. This is where sequence shows up.

While 36.5 inches of rain does fall in a year, only 100 days have rain. More importantly, the rainy days tend to be clustered in the June-October time frame.

If a person was expecting 0.1 inches of rain every day, then he might never turn on his sprinkler system and all of his grass and flowers would wither and die in the months between November and May.

Obviously this is a bad idea if you want to enjoy a healthy garden. It's also a bad idea if you want a healthy portfolio. If you expected a certain percentage return every year, your portfolio will quickly turn to dust.

While the long-run average return of the U.S. stock markets has been around 8%, that in no way guarantees a return of 8% every year. It is entirely possible that an investor can experience very high returns early in their growth investment years (say, the 1990s) and low or even negative returns near the end of their growth investment years (like the late 2000s).

The timing of the returns becomes everything.

If high returns are earned early on, then investors feel more confident as they watch their portfolios explode to the upside. They start to feel richer and plan for a more comfortable retirement.

Then, when the down years hit near the end, the investor is faced with a double whammy. Not only are the bad years draining his retirement account, but the number of years left to work and make up the losses is dwindling.

The solution is to understand that average is important, but sequence — the order in which returns are earned — is paramount.

This requires investors to understand and forecast what lies ahead. It's hard, but it can help investors save a lifetime of accumulated assets.

Think about those who were on the cusp of retirement in 2007, 2008 and even 2009. If they were relying on market averages to see them through, then they most likely left their retirement accounts exposed to great risk near the end of their working careers.

As the markets cratered, investors in this situation saw their IRAs, 401ks and other accounts lose value by the minute.

While the "average" told them to expect 8%, the sequence led to massive losses just when they could not afford it.

Knowing the importance of sequence, you should examine exactly how much risk you are taking and what potentially lies ahead. With the global economy clearly in slowdown mode, now is not the time to be taking risk, especially if you can't afford sequential years of low or negative returns.

Besides... who wants to be average?

Baby Boomers are Retiring

October, 2012

"I want the truth!"

"You can't handle the truth!"

It seems like we, the American people, are desperately screaming at the television this election season, just like Tom Cruise screamed at Jack Nicholson in the classic A Few Good Men. We want the presidential candidates to drop their posturing and just tell us the truth… about the economy and how exactly they intend to fix it.

Of course, Romney and Obama never give an answer. They just spout more platitudes and generalities like, "I'll lower taxes and businesses will spend more," which has not worked. Or, "I've saved millions of jobs, we just need more tax money to spend," which is also a non-starter.

It's as if they think we don't know what's right before our eyes — a weak economy that shows no signs of this wondrous recovery they keep alluding to.

They tell us to believe all their promises… if only we elect them then things will be all sunshine and roses.

Well, I've got news for them…

It is not us, the workers and taxpayers of America, that are dazed and confused. It's Mr. Romney and President Obama… and their ill-fated advisors.

To turn the phrase around, it is not that Americans "can't handle the truth." It's that the politicians refuse to acknowledge the truth!

So, today I give you what the frank, clear discussion of our economic situation should be about. And, for good measure, I throw in some broad examples of what we can do to start moving our economy forward.

Why Stagnation Lies Ahead

The long-term forecast today is for a period of stagnation. Why? Because the largest group in our economy, the baby boomers, are paying off debts. They're preparing for retirement. This type of activity doesn't lead to strong GDP growth where problems like unemployment take care of themselves.

Just as the boomers spent aggressively to grow their families from the early 1980s through the mid-2000s, which led to an amazing run of debt-fueled growth in the country, they now hold back. They refuse to budge when enticed with low interest rates or other fiscal stimulus.

The reason for the change is clear: baby boomers now have different goals. It is no longer about the biggest house or newest car. It's about preparing for a comfortable retirement, or even any retirement at all.

With this new reality staring us in the face, what can our political candidates do?

For starters, they can work to understand their constituents and acknowledge the major financial concerns people have. They must recognize the current economic Winter Season that baby boomers have created as they move into their saving years.

Next, Mr. Romney and President Obama et al could clearly identify what won't work in the years ahead. Enticing consumers to spend their every last nickel AND incur more debt won't jumpstart the economy.

In fact, every time I hear someone say that lower interest rates will make everything okay it makes me want to scream!

How in the world can piling more debt onto consumers fix an economy that is weighed down by too much debt? This is so idiotic a 10-year-old could point out the flaws.

If we can just set aside this failed idea, then perhaps we can have a discussion of what might work to help lower unemployment... to balance the books of our states and country. We have some suggestions...

Fix America Step #1:
Recognize Why Enticements Won't Help

If everyone has a DVD player and the price of DVD players fall to $1, how many more would sell? Not many!

Sure, people will buy some as replacements, or perhaps to have one in another room of the home, but there wouldn't be a surge of demand.

This is where we are in the economy, but the "good" in question is not a DVD player, it's debt.

The boomers, that huge mass of people in our economy, already have all the debt they want and then some. Simply forcing down interest rates or easing credit will not have the hoped for positive affect.

In fact, this "enticement" has more of a negative affect…

When the Fed holds down interest rates, savers and those on fixed incomes feel the pain.

The exact actions being taken to boost the economy are what are making it even worse. Brilliant!

Fix America Step #2:
Raise Tax Rates

There are no two-ways about this one. The lower consumption and higher savings trends prevalent in our economy today constrain growth. This, of course, cuts into any sort of growth of tax revenue as well.

There will have to be higher taxes. The Bowles-Simpson report is a good model for this, where tax increases are affected by vastly reducing or even eliminating deductions, while at the same time lowering marginal rates and the corporate tax rate.

As a side note, there will have to be a mechanism for transmitting sales tax on Internet purchases back to the consumer's state of residency. Today billions of dollars in sales tax are not collected, even though voters agreed to this tax mechanism.

Now, no one wants to pay more taxes. But most people I meet do want to be responsible. They understand taxes might have to rise, but before they pay another nickel they want to know that all the money sent to the government is being spent responsibly. This makes sense.

Fix America Step #3:
Spending Will Have to Fall

Again, Bowles-Simpson has a good plan, but we think adding in some suggestions by Rep. Coburn's "Back in Black" report will make it better.

The general notion is to raise the bar for entitlement payments… to critically review current government spending. One area that we highlighted in our latest book, The Great Crash Ahead, was U.S. military bases maintained in foreign countries. Certainly the presence of tens of thousands of American soldiers in Germany is not as necessary today as it might have been in previous decades.

Fix America Step #4:
Housing Is Not the Issue, It's Debt

The estimates of underwater homes — those that are worth less than the mortgage outstanding — vary, but are always large. Whether the number is 11 million homes or 12 million doesn't matter.

The U.S. housing market is in a deep freeze because of two huge forces. First, demographically the baby boomers bought their trade up homes in their early 40s, pushing up demand from the late 1990s through the mid-2000s.

The group behind them, the Gen X'ers, is smaller, so demand softens naturally.

Second, the big run up attracted easy credit and speculation, which turned a naturally rising industry into a bubble. Now the bubble has burst and is deflating. This is a very long and very painful process.

It can be done — albeit still with pain — quickly, which will help the economy heal faster. This would require either an equity-sharing plan as we outlined in our book, where lenders take equity in lieu of a portion of mortgages, or something like the imminent domain plan being considered in California.

Both would require a breach of mortgage contracts. The question is, "How long do we want the housing pain to continue?" What is it worth to solve this thorny issue sooner rather than later?

There are several other suggestions we could tell the presidential candidates about... but none of them are easy. That's why we don't think Mr. Romney and President Obama really want to hear the truth. They just want to win an election.

Why Are We Still Working?!?

February, 2013

"Oh Lord, won't you buy me a Mercedes Benz. My friends all have Porches, I must make amends."

That song lyric by Janis Joplin runs through my head every time I see all these Fed-apologist pundits on TV and in the paper. They keep telling us that if only we printed a lot more money, and heaven forbid don't stop what we are printing now, the economy will recover and life will be glorious!

Really?!

Is it that easy?

If it's so darn easy to ensure prosperity, then WHY AM I STILL WORKING?! And why are YOU still working?! Why do ANY of us keep working?!

I mean, if Mr. Krugman and Mr. Blinder et al are correct, then printing money out of thin air has no consequence. There are no bad outcomes. The money just magically flows into the broad economy and all is good.

If they are to be believed, then why in the world is anyone in the U.S. still putting in a 9-to-5? Why are we not simply receiving a check, or electronic transfer from the Fed and then kicking back?

After all, it wouldn't be that hard...

Currently there are roughly 212 million adults in the U.S. If everyone needs a couple of million dollars to be comfortable, then the Fed can simply print $424 trillion. And it can send each of these funds via tax refund because the IRS knows where everyone is anyway, right?

And speaking of the IRS, after they've sent along our newly printed dollars, just disband them. Who needs them?

If money can be printed with zero consequences, then just print it and ship it to the U.S. Treasury to fund government operations. What do they need a year, $16 trillion? No problem!

Of course it doesn't work.

It would mean people have money without providing productivity on the other side. Money for nothing. When money is traded for nothing, eventually the money is worth nothing.

The problem is it's not just the new money, printed and exchanged for nothing, that becomes worthless. When this sort of wild printing takes place all of the currency loses value. It puts goods and services out of reach of the average person by making that person's savings and wages worth nothing.

The bad news is that this is the path the Fed is on right now.

The good news is they won't get there.

The Fed has been as focused as possible on stealing value from savers and giving it to those who trade in U.S. government bonds, eventually handing tens of billions of dollars to the U.S. Treasury. This process has stopped what would have been a normally deflating economy. But it has left ugly side effects behind...

The newly printed money is not distributed to all Americans. It is sent to just a few. Yet, ALL of us pay higher prices for food, energy, education and health care. This mismatch, where some get the benefit but all get the pain, is the source of great frustration in the U.S. today.

Several members of the Fed Open Market Committee are talking about this issue, and we anticipate the Fed slowing and ending its programs long before high levels of inflation return.

Unfortunately, every day that goes by with more printing of new dollars and falling wages of Average Americans is a day too many. We are watching our standard of living fade one day at a time. That is, unless you have the ability to call upon a higher power to send you a Mercedes Benz, flat screen plasma TV, and a night on the town.

So far, those prayers aren't being answered, and Ben Bernanke isn't mailing me any checks.

Darn it.

Every Man for Himself

January, 2014

Justo Rodriguez is a Spaniard who has a problem. Six years ago he mortgaged his property and his father's property to install solar panels.

He did that because the Spanish government promised to pay anyone who generated electricity from renewable sources a guaranteed rate for the next 25 years.

A little math showed Justo that the amount of electricity he could generate would pay all the mortgages on a monthly basis as well as provide extra income. This was an annuity arbitrage. Right up until the government backed out of the deal…

The Spanish government has greatly reduced the rate it will pay producers of electricity from renewable sources, and is even considering charging them for their effect on traditional energy companies.

The new math of the situation bankrupts Justo, leaving him and his father broke and homeless.

This is what can happen when people rely on one source of income. And it's not just something that happens across the pond, in a country reeling from a credit implosion. It happens right here. Just ask retirees in Pritchard, Alabama; Central Falls, Rhode Island; and now those in Detroit, Michigan.

Each of the cities listed above had made pension promises. Over time, it became obvious they could not pay those pensions. Yet each city continued to send money out the door, year after year, sometimes noting that the path was unsustainable… sometimes not.

Both Pritchard and Central Falls have had to cut or simply eliminate some pension payments, leaving those who were relying on them to fend for themselves. Retirees in Detroit are facing the ugly prospect of defending their claims on the city as just one more unsecured creditor. Good luck with that.

A quick calculation of Detroit's assets and liabilities show that retirees are in line to get about 30 cents on the dollar. It probably won't end up that bad, but it won't be pretty.

When it comes to retirement promises, the federal government is just as guilty of unilateral changes as the towns above. When Social Security was passed it was supposed to be voluntary, it was never going to be taxed, and the funds were never going to be commingled with the general funds of the U.S. That didn't work out so well.

In the early 1970s, inflation was eating away at the purchasing power of Social Security payments, so Congress voted to add cost-of-living adjustments, or COLAs. Every year, Social Security payments are adjusted to reflect the change in the consumer price index (CPI) from the previous year (unless it fell, but that's a different story).

The point is to allow those who receive Social Security to maintain their standard of living, however meager it might be.

Now the government is working to change this calculation from the move in CPI to the move in chained-CPI, which is a measure of how wages have changed in the previous year.

Given that wages, adjusted for inflation, have actually fallen for half a decade and are now back to the levels of the mid-1990s, this change doesn't bode well for retirees.

The point is that, just like in Spain and Central Falls, Rhode Island, there is no "iron clad, always will be paid, never to be broken" contract. Even with the U.S. government.

There is always a way for the other party to pay less or simply not pay at all... especially if the other party controls the legislature and the judiciary.

For those of us who have to plan our retirement, trying to develop ways to pay for decades out of the workforce, not being able to rely on counterparties makes things difficult. It means we have to find more than one source of income, never relying too heavily on one group or company, and never falling for the word "guaranteed."

And it means continuing to read Survive & Prosper and Boom & Bust because we're all about helping you find ways to make extra income without breaking the bank or your back, or risking everything.

PENSIONS

Pensions That Kill

May, 2012

Safeway Stores owes more in unfunded pension liabilities than the entire company is worth. The city of Providence, Rhode Island will most likely follow Central Falls, Rhode Island into bankruptcy to greatly reduce its pension liabilities. American Airlines is fighting with the Pension Benefit Guaranty Corporation (PBGC) over who will pay for $8 billion in unfunded pensions. Notice a trend?

Whether in business or the public sector, most organizations that have been around a while will have pension obligations. Most likely, they also have health care obligations to their retirees.

The system that brought these liabilities into existence — great benefits, early retirement and a shortage of labor — belongs to another era, namely the late '40s and '50s. The system that must pay for these liabilities is the one we have today and cut-throat competition, falling wages and no financial wiggle room are the order of the day.

So what is the answer to this "pensions problem"? To punt, of course. Or, in this case, file for bankruptcy protection from your debts.

In some instances, cities, states or companies reduce their pension obligations, like Central Falls in Rhode Island did. But such practice is not the norm. Instead, cities like Vallejo in California, that had a huge pension issue, simply declared bankruptcy. They went to court and eventually emerged with a settlement that saw vendor payments, not pensions, were reduced. This means the taxpayers in Vallejo still owe the pensions.

On the private company side, American Airlines might be able to foist its pensions onto the PBGC, but what does that mean? Given that the PBGC is a public entity, it means U.S. taxpayers are on the hook for any shortfall. The PBGC already has billions in deficit, so what's $8 billion more?

The point is that pension liabilities are killing the country one city and one company at a time. When revenues and expenses aren't allowed to fluctuate together, any system will eventually break down. If a company wants to offer pension, it should look no further than buying the right amount of U.S. Treasury bonds that mature in the correct years to pay the liabilities when they come due. Anything short of this puts future cash flow at risk…which is where we are today.

The current estimate is that cities and states are roughly $1 trillion underfunded in their pension and health care liabilities. Corporate America is underfunded by roughly $400 billion.

Think of the millions of current and future retirees that are counting on this income. Now think of how much it will cost you and me as the American taxpayer to make good on all these promises.

The only thing I know for sure is that taxes can only go up from here. And no one flourishes under a heavy tax burden. In the next few years, we will have to work a lot harder, making good investment decisions and squirreling away as much money as you can.

Don't Go Down With Your Pension Fund

March, 2012

"You've all just made the biggest mistake of your lives."

"You're gonna die on this plane. It's gonna crash."

"The company is bankrupt and this plane is going down with all of you on it."

Then a first class passenger tackled her to the floor just to shut her up.

Ok… we don't know *exactly* what this crazed flight attendant said over the PA system on the American Airlines flight to Chicago on March 9. But we'd imagine there were additional, juicy expletives peppered in there. Especially if she'd recently read the American Airlines bankruptcy filing that revealed the company's pension plan is $18 billion underfunded.

She's not alone in her concerns, although she's alone in voicing her hysteria publicly.

Recently General Electric (GE) calculated what it must put aside to fund its pension this year. They were surprised to discover their required payment for this year is $7 billion more than they thought it would be.

That's not chump-change. That's not even a minor miscalculation. That's downright shocking.

So what changed? How did they get it so wrong?

Quite simply, they had to factor in the effect of the Fed's efforts to keep interest rates at historic lows.

Low Interest Rates Have Knocked the Comfort Out of Pensions

Every year, companies crunch the numbers to see how much they must set aside for that year to meet their long-term pension obligations. Part of this calculation involves using interest rates to estimate how money will compound over time.

The interest rates and the required payments have an inverse relationship. If interest rates are high, the company assumes the pension will have high earnings thanks to investments in interest-bearing securities. This means the company needs to contribute less money to the pension plan.

If interest rates are low, then the opposite is true and the company must contribute more funds to the pension.

Currently, with short term interest rates at 0.25%, they are at rock bottom. So companies like GE, Boeing and American Airlines must suddenly make insanely high pension contributions.

Where does the money come from? Earnings, of course. And that's the rub.

Companies have decided that using money to fund pensions is a real drag on earnings. So they've petitioned the Senate for a reprieve. After all, they're thinking "Who needs to fund pesky pensions anyway? Won't interest rates go up soon enough? Aren't those liabilities a long way off?"

Senators are actually considering this exemption because less pension contributions would mean more taxable income and therefore more tax. In their minds it's a win-win deal.

Except it isn't.

It's a win-win-lose situation. The company may win by contributing less. Congress may win by getting more tax income. But the worker, the pensioner, loses because his pension won't be fully funded when his retirement rolls around. He faces a pauper's retirement thanks to corporate and Senate short-sightedness.

The Redundancy Plan is Dead in the Water

It gets worse.

The Pension Benefit Guarantee Corporation (PBGC), the government entity that's meant to take over pensions from failed companies, is tens of billions underfunded. It's in no position to ensure the pensioner gets his dues. And that's not the worst part. The PBGC does not really pay out what a pensioner is owed from his company. Instead it pays out a very modest, barebones amount based on its own calculations of length of service and pay.

Pensions across America are in a nose dive. Are you willing to bet your financial future on the goodwill of a company and Congress?

Me either.

That's why, if you have a pension, look through your company's quarterly filings to determine how well funded it is. There is a good chance you will be staring at a bad surprise.

If you are going to maintain your standard of living in retirement, you need to take several steps to prepare yourself now. Add income streams to your portfolio. Increase your savings. And be prepared to grab opportunities to short the market when the time comes.

Pensioners, Welcome to Ben Bernanke's House of Pain

June, 2012

The bad news for pensioners just doesn't stop.

In 2009, the Pew Center issued a report called "The $1 Trillion Funding Gap." The report estimated that city, state and local pensions (collectively referred to as public pensions) and retirement benefits were underfunded by $1 trillion. That was a big number. And now it's bigger.

The Pew Center just issued an update. Between 2009 and 2011, the funding gap exploded from $1 trillion to $1.4 trillion! Cities, counties and states are not filling up their pension funds, they're falling behind in what they owe.

One group we can blame for this is politicians...

Legislators at all levels have avoided making the hard decisions required to properly fund pensions.

It's not as if no one knows about the problem. We've been writing about it since 2006. City and state governments have held talks on the subject since the 1990s. But no one ever did anything about it.

Now, after the Great Recession and while we are still in the economic Winter Season, people are paying attention. Cities like Providence and Central Falls in Rhode Island, Pritchard in Alabama and Vallejo in California are just a few examples of towns laid low by the pensions they owe.

Some declare bankruptcy. Others, like Central Falls, tell their current retirees — people who are already retired — that they will take a huge cut in pension payments. Immediately. Still others, like Pritchard, simply quit paying anything at all.

The city of San Diego, which we outlined in our last book The Great Crash Ahead, made successive bad deals with its pension funds and has recently forced its employees to pay in more while accepting lower benefits.

Ben's House of Pain

But the pain doesn't stop with falling benefits and higher require payments. There's also the other side of the funds — what states earn. For the pain on this side of the coin, thank Ben Bernanke.

We have pointed out time and again that no monetary action comes without pain. The entire reason for taking action is to move wealth from one group to another... to give one group a benefit at another group's expense. Well, if you're an investor, if you're a pensioner, welcome to Ben's House of Pain.

On June 20, the Federal Reserve announced the continuation of Operation Twist, where the Fed will sell its short maturity Treasury bonds (those maturing in less than three years). It will use the money to buy long maturity Treasury bonds.

The goal is clearly to keep interest rates low and even force them lower. Who does it help? Borrowers, of course! Why else would 30-year mortgages currently be at 3.53% while inflation is 2.3%? This is the lowest mortgage rates have ever been in history!

The Fed is engineering lower rates to favor borrowers, which by definition means that it's punishing savers, both individuals like you and me AND institutions like pension funds that rely on fixed income to meet their long-term liabilities.

So those same cities, counties and states that have not put enough money aside to pay their obligations to retirees are now seeing what little they do have set aside earn a pittance!

What's the Solution?

There is one, but you won't like it. Because YOU are the solution. Well, at least your money is.

When it comes to unfunded liabilities, there aren't many choices. Tax your citizens more. Require higher payments from workers. Reduce benefits. Extend out the eligibility age (which is another way of reducing benefits). All of these things take wealth from people to put it in the hands of government so that they can meet at least some of their obligations.

This is not a pretty situation, and given the state of the economy, expect things to get worse, not better.

This is where you get to make a choice. Do you sit idly by and watch your pension checks and other funds dwindle, or do you take a stand and become proactive?

Start building your own future today. Take steps to build income streams wherever you can. Strong dividend-paying companies are a good place to look, but know that the equity price will likely underperform for many years. Don't expect to make your money on capital gains.

Another way to build income streams is to stay agile in the market. Be prepared to take advantage of a bust ahead, by selling short a particular equity. And be ready to jump on board a boom.

Finally, make the cash you bring in through those income streams work for you. Find the highest yielding, safest places to put your dollars. Utility bonds are a good place to park your cash. EverBank's High Yield Money Market Account, with its promise of a 1.06 average percentage yield and a bonus rate of 1.35%, is another good place for your money.

Unless you take action now, you can kiss your retirement goodbye.